Whether you have ever personally had to confront the dreaded reality of a cancer diagnosis, or comfort a friend or loved one through his or her fight against cancer, your possession of this book is not happenstance.

Along our life's journey, our humanness at times causes us to defocus from the promises of God as revealed to us in the Scriptures. *A Season for Hope* provides an awakening-by-awakening refocus, in personal letter format, on many of the promises available to fellow believers.

I recommend *A Season for Hope* to people of all faiths, and I thank Dr. Barry for making it available to all of us.

From the foreword
by ROGER CARY
PRESIDENT AND CEO
CANCER TREATMENT CENTERS OF AMERICA

Also by Michael S. Barry

A REASON FOR HOPE
Gaining Strength for Your Fight Against Cancer

A SEASON for HOPE

DAILY ENCOURAGEMENT *for* Your FIGHT AGAINST CANCER

MICHAEL S. BARRY

Honor® is an imprint of
Cook Communications Ministries, Colorado Springs, CO 80918
Cook Communications, Paris, Ontario
Kingsway Communications, Eastbourne, England

A SEASON FOR HOPE
Copyright © 2005 by Michael S. Barry

Published in association with the literary agency of Les Stobbe, 300 Doubleday Rd., Tyron, NC 28782

Cover Design by Greg Jackson, Jackson Design Co, llc
Cover Photo © Digital Vision

First printing, 2005
Printed in the United States of America
Printing/Year
10 9 8 7 6 5 4 3 2 / 05 06 07 08 09

Unless otherwise noted, Scripture quotations are taken from the HOLY BIBLE, NEW INTERNATIONAL VERSION®. Copyright © 1973, 1978, 1984 International Bible Society. Used by permission of Zondervan. All rights reserved. Scripture quotations marked MSG are taken from The Message. Copyright © by Eugene H. Peterson, 2002. Used by permission of NavPress Publishing Group. Other Scripture taken from the Authorized (King James) Version of the Bible (KJV). Italics in Scripture are added by the author for emphasis.

Library of Congress Cataloging-in-Publication Data

Barry, Michael S., 1952-
    A season for hope / Michael S. Barry.
        p. cm.
    Includes bibliographical references.
    ISBN 1-56292-283-1 (pbk.)
    1. Cancer--Patients--Religious life. 2. Cancer--Religious aspects--Christianity. I. Title.
    BV4910.33.B384 2005
    248.8'6196994--dc22

                            2004026676

Contents

FOREWORD
by Roger Cary, President & CEO
Cancer Treatment Centers of America 7
INTRODUCTION 9
CHAPTER 1: A FRIEND WHO UNDERSTANDS 11
CHAPTER 2: THE DEVASTATION OF DIAGNOSIS 13
CHAPTER 3: SCIENTIFIC INFORMATION—TOO LITTLE
AND TOO MUCH 15
CHAPTER 4: LONELINESS ON THE EDGE OF HELL 19
CHAPTER 5: GOD NEITHER SLUMBERS NOR
SLEEPS 21
CHAPTER 6: FREEDOM FROM NEGATIVITY 23
CHAPTER 7: FORGIVENESS AND PEACE 25
CHAPTER 8: CONNECTING THE EMOTIONAL DOTS 29
CHAPTER 9: CHOOSING TO FIGHT 33
CHAPTER 10: UNNECESSARY UNHAPPINESS 35
CHAPTER 11: STEALERS OF HOPE 39
CHAPTER 12: NO TIME FOR VANITY 43
CHAPTER 13: CHRONIC NICENESS 47
CHAPTER 14: A "CAN-DO" ATTITUDE 49
CHAPTER 15: A QUESTION OF BALANCE 51
CHAPTER 16: LIVING WITH CANCER.....................53
CHAPTER 17: GOD'S RENEWING POWER 55
CHAPTER 18: THE GIFT OF HEALING 57
CHAPTER 19: A MIND-SET FOR MIRACLES.................61
CHAPTER 20: AN UNSATISFYING ANSWER.................63
CHAPTER 21: POSITIVE THINKING 67
CHAPTER 22: THE INEVITABILITY OF PAIN 69
CHAPTER 23: THE PATIENT AS TEACHER 71
CHAPTER 24: THE SPIRIT OF HOPE 73
CHAPTER 25: THE IMPORTANCE OF HOPE 75
CHAPTER 26: THE GREATEST OF THESE IS HOPE......79
CHAPTER 27: THE SOURCE OF HOPE.....................83

CHAPTER 28: THE BEST THING 87

CHAPTER 29: THE LESSONS OF SUFFERING 89

CHAPTER 30: FIGHTING EVIL 93

CHAPTER 31: GOD'S PREVENIENT GRACE 95

CHAPTER 32: THE COMFORT OF SCRIPTURE 97

CHAPTER 33: SUSPICION OF THE GIFT OF
    HEALING 101

CHAPTER 34: GOOD AND ANGRY 105

CHAPTER 35: MOOD SWINGS OF EXHAUSTION 109

CHAPTER 36: ORDAINED TO BE A FRIEND 111

CHAPTER 37: MIRACLES OF SPONTANEOUS
    REMISSION 113

CHAPTER 38: A PRISON OF DEPRESSION 117

CHAPTER 39: PRAYER AS MEDICAL PROTOCOL 121

CHAPTER 40: BE. DO. HAVE. 125

CHAPTER 41: THE UNFAIRNESS OF IT ALL 129

CHAPTER 42: TRUST BUT VERIFY 133

CHAPTER 43: SIZE DOESN'T MATTER 137

CHAPTER 44: THE REAL PROBLEM 141

CHAPTER 45: FOOTPRINTS OF FAITH 145

CHAPTER 46: THE FAITH-HEALTH CONNECTION 149

CHAPTER 47: PATIENCE—SIMPLE, REALLY 151

CHAPTER 48: RECONNECTING WITH GOD 153

CHAPTER 49: GETTING UP WHEN YOU'RE DOWN 157

CHAPTER 50: PERMISSION TO BE HUMAN 161

CHAPTER 51: MEDICAL NEGLIGENCE 165

CHAPTER 52: THE AROMA OF CHRIST 167

CHAPTER 53: FIGHTING FOR LIFE BUT OBEDIENT
    TO DEATH 171

CHAPTER 54: THE LITMUS TEST OF LOVE 173

CHAPTER 55: SINGING THE LORD'S SONG 175

CHAPTER 56: PRAYER THAT RISKS 179

CHAPTER 57: IF THE END APPEARS NEAR 183

CHAPTER 58: LAST WORDS 187

NOTES 190

Many believe that God places people in our path when we need them most. Whether you have ever personally had to confront the dreaded reality of a cancer diagnosis, or comfort a friend or loved one through his or her fight against cancer, your possession of this book is not happenstance.

In my capacity as chief operating officer of Cancer Treatment Centers of America and as president and CEO of Midwestern Regional Medical Center, I am privileged to observe and support our chaplain, Rev. Dr. Michael S. Barry, in his ministry to patients of all faiths from every state in our nation and from many foreign countries.

As you may expect, most of our patients are followers of Christianity or other faiths, and I am always eager to learn what they value in terms of our spiritual presence in their lives. When battling cancer, where do they find their strength? Where do they go? How do they cope? What role will their faith play in their treatment and possible healing?

Happily for them and for all of us, *A Season for Hope* was written from the heart of an authentic, compassionate caregiver. Dr. Barry truly understands the strength available to those of our patients who embrace the Christian faith. "Because we know the road ahead and its glorious destination," he once said, "our reason for hope is made certain."

Along our life's journey, our humanness at times causes us to defocus from the promises of God as revealed to us in the

Scriptures. *A Season for Hope* provides an awakening-by-awakening refocus, in personal letter format, on many of the promises available to fellow believers.

I am impressed by the wonderful array of empowering spiritual insights presented in this book. Of course, Dr. Barry does not suggest that we abandon all the progress that medical science has made; he simply reminds us that we become certain of the victory that is ours when we also place our faith in the heavenly Father. Philippians 4:13 promises, "I can do everything through him who gives me strength."

So what can you expect to take away from a book about the hope that we as Christians have? Not just encouraging, true stories (though you'll find some very good ones). Not just scriptural promises (though they are abundant). Not just success tips on how one may deal with cancer (though they are freely given). In this powerful little book you will find hundreds of insights focusing on friendship, family, and the celebration of life—all derived from authentic faith in God.

I recommend *A Season for Hope* to people of all faiths, and I thank Dr. Barry for making it available to all of us.

ROGER CARY

PRESIDENT AND CEO

CANCER TREATMENT CENTERS OF AMERICA

INTRODUCTION

I am an insider. God has given me opportunities to sit quietly with people whose lives have been turned upside down by cancer. Often these meetings have occurred behind closed doors, in the privacy of a patient's room. Sometimes I have met with patients one-on-one, other times with close friends or family members present, and other times in a group. Sometimes we have met tearfully, sometimes joyfully, sometimes hopefully. There have been times when people seemed to have one foot already in heaven and other times when the future was brightened by reports of remission. I may not have seen it all, but I have enough experience to be considered an insider in the hearts and minds of people who suffer with cancer.

These dear people share every feeling, every hope, and every dream with me. I listen to them and they listen to me, and together we develop personal relationships that transcend my role as a caregiver and theirs as patients. I have learned that while formal roles have their benefits, too often they inhibit deep friendships from developing at a time when they are needed the most.

This book is intended to be a companion. I've written in the intimate style of a series of personal letters, and my expectation is that you, the reader, will sense that in me you have a friend—someone who understands you and is as available as you want me to be.

I fully expect that as you read this book you will gain a greater appreciation for the benefits of true friendship. There is no replacement for knowing someone who truly understands what you are going through. And although I may not know you personally, that doesn't mean that I am not your friend. If you are a Christian, you are not only a friend, but you are also family. If you are not a Christian, we are united by our common humanity, and I desire to be your friend as well. If you need to contact me, please do so.

And now, my friend,

May the God of peace, who through the blood of the eternal covenant brought back from the dead our Lord Jesus, that great Shepherd of the sheep, equip you with everything good for doing his will, and may he work in us what is pleasing to him, through Jesus Christ, to whom be glory for ever and ever. Amen.

HEBREWS 13:20–21

MICHAEL S. BARRY
HOPE-BOOKS.COM

CHAPTER ONE

A Friend Who Understands

---◆---

"I NO LONGER CALL YOU SERVANTS, BECAUSE A SERVANT
DOES NOT KNOW HIS MASTER'S BUSINESS. INSTEAD, I HAVE CALLED
YOU FRIENDS, FOR EVERYTHING THAT I LEARNED FROM MY
FATHER I HAVE MADE KNOWN TO YOU."

JOHN 15:15

Dear friend:
    In my letters to you I refer to you as "friend." I do this because I believe it is the best name I could give you, the holiest, most endearing term I know of to define the contours of our relationship. Because friendship—with Christ—is the pinnacle of intimacy with God, friendship ought also to characterize the relationships among His disciples.

A good portion of my doctoral dissertation was on the topic of friendship. I have learned that friendship includes certain expectations and behaviors, such as unconditional love and forgiveness. But studies have shown that what we really want from our best friends is *to be understood*.

This is what you want from *your* friends right now. You want them to know and accept your deepest feelings, to understand your fears and confusions and the nature of your disease. You want them to understand your need for love and hope, your sense of losing control of your life, and the pain that often comes with feeling powerless. You want them to understand *you*—and what you are going through.

As a fellow Christian, you are my friend. I may not know you personally now, or ever in this lifetime, but eternity is our shared future. If I can do or say anything to help you cope with and overcome your cancer, I want to be available to you. I may not know you, but if you have cancer, I understand you, and that makes you my friend.

Lord Jesus, I am united in friendship with You, through the power and workings of the Holy Spirit in my life. You have connected me to others—very special people—whom You love and adore. Help me to help them by understanding their worries and concerns, their hopes and dreams. In Jesus' name I pray. Amen.

CHAPTER TWO

The Devastation of Diagnosis

---◆---

OBSESSION WITH SELF IN THESE MATTERS
IS A DEAD END; ATTENTION TO GOD LEADS US OUT INTO
THE OPEN, INTO A SPACIOUS, FREE LIFE.

ROMANS 8:6 (MSG)

Dear friend:
Let me see if I have your story straight. Recently you began to bleed from your intestines every time you went to the bathroom. You were frightened. You began to panic. You called everyone you knew. The next day you had a colonoscopy and were told that a tumor in your colon had probably been there for three or four years. Two days later you were assigned a surgeon and scheduled for surgery. You were so panic-stricken that you didn't even know what questions to ask. Now, after your surgery, you are here in the hospital receiving a combination of chemotherapy and radiation for an indefinite period of time.

If that, or something close to it, is your story, I cannot even begin to imagine how sad you must feel—not to mention all the other feelings you're having. In only a short span of time your world has been completely turned upside down. You've lost control of your life. Your future plans have been put on hold. Your life as you knew it has come to an immediate stop. You must feel as though you have been in a car accident or a train wreck. Sadness is the feeling we have when we experience *loss*, and you've lost a good deal—particularly control over your life.

I encourage you to resist the temptation to become obsessed with your situation. It leads to a dead end. You do have some control left in your life, and that has to do with what you pay attention to, what you allow your mind to focus on. As the Scriptures teach us, "Attention to God leads us out into the open, into a spacious, free life."

Now is the time for you to learn from your experiences. Others have gone through what you are going through and survived. Those who do survive often experience spiritual renewal as they sense God's goodness and love overpowering this disease we call cancer.

I invite you to calm down as much as you can. Relax. Your healing will take some time. Allow God to work in and through the doctors, nutritionists, and other caregivers and their treatment. Allow God to bless you during this time of need in your life.

Lord Jesus, cancer can be a whirlwind—devastating, destructive, life-changing. As my friend tries to pick up the pieces of his life, help him not to focus on all that is negative, but rather to focus his mind on You and all that is being done for him by so many others. Lead him into the open, into a spacious, cancer-free life. In Your name I pray. Amen.

CHAPTER THREE

Scientific Information—
Too Little and Too Much

❖

DEAR FRIEND, TAKE MY ADVICE;

IT WILL ADD YEARS TO YOUR LIFE.

I'M WRITING OUT CLEAR DIRECTIONS TO WISDOM WAY,

I'M DRAWING A MAP TO RIGHTEOUS ROAD.

I DON'T WANT YOU ENDING UP IN BLIND ALLEYS,

OR WASTING TIME MAKING WRONG TURNS.

HOLD TIGHT TO GOOD ADVICE; DON'T RELAX YOUR GRIP.

GUARD IT WELL—YOUR LIFE IS AT STAKE!

DON'T TAKE WICKED BYPASS;

DON'T SO MUCH AS SET FOOT ON THAT ROAD.

STAY CLEAR OF IT; GIVE IT A WIDE BERTH.

MAKE A DETOUR AND BE ON YOUR WAY.

PROVERBS 4:10–15 (MSG)

D ear friend:

Even as King Solomon had *life-giving* advice to share with his friend, I am convinced that I too have advice that has the possibility of adding years to your life. I am not being arrogant. I am not trying to make you feel better by giving you false hope. I don't believe for a minute that lying to you about your situation is in your best interest. You deserve to know the truth, and I am sure you would not want our relationship to be based on lies and misinformation. What I am offering you are simply a couple of facts that you need to know. I believe that they will lead you along "Wisdom Way" to longer life, health, and peace.

- **Predictions made by well-meaning doctors are frequently incorrect.** I regularly teach a class called Spirituality and Health to cancer patients, many of whom have been told by their initial oncology experts that they have no hope; that they should go home, get their affairs in order, and die. The truth is that many people live significantly longer—years, in fact—than their doctors' predictions. Do not believe anyone who tells you that you have X number of days, months, or years to live. Your future is in God's hands—God's alone—and no one has the right to strip either of us of our hope.

- **There is so much new information about cancer and how to treat it that many doctors find themselves almost paralyzed by the glut of new information, uncertain about what to do next for their patients.** Occasionally I teach Spirituality and Health seminars to doctors and other medical professionals, and I begin by referring to the information glut, which I learned about in an article in the *New England Journal of Medicine:*

The yawning chasm between what we know and what we do for patients is no longer news; indeed the reported evidence is somewhat numbing. We are far less sure what to do next.[1]

I have a tremendous amount of respect and empathy for the medical profession. How in the world is it possible to stay on top of all of the latest developments in cancer treatment? Our doctors deserve our understanding and prayers. Often only the best and brightest are privileged to enter the field of medicine, and they are nearly always the threshold to the door of our healing.

Here's the truth I ask you to consider: Modern research is completely rewriting the statistics on cancer to the end that it is now considered to be a *chronic* disease, like diabetes, instead of a *fatal* disease. The survival rates continue to climb. Can it be fatal? Of course. Is there hope that you can either learn to live with your cancer or be cured of it? Yes, I believe there is, because I am around people all the time who have beaten the odds. Why not you?

Lord, help my friend to put her trust in You. Today, lead her toward "Righteous Road," and help her steer clear of "Wicked Bypass," which leads only to pessimism, self-defeating attitudes, and hopelessness. In Jesus' name I pray. Amen.

---❖---

THE PSALMIST WAS ABLE
TO MAKE IT THROUGH HIS LIVING HELL
BECAUSE GOD DID NOT ABANDON HIM.

CHAPTER FOUR

Loneliness on the Edge of Hell

◆

GOD, YOU'RE MY LAST CHANCE OF THE DAY.

I SPEND THE NIGHT ON MY KNEES BEFORE YOU.

PUT ME ON YOUR SALVATION AGENDA;

TAKE NOTES ON THE TROUBLE I'M IN.

I'VE HAD MY FILL OF TROUBLE;

I'M CAMPED ON THE EDGE OF HELL.

I'M WRITTEN OFF AS A LOST CAUSE,

ONE MORE STATISTIC, A HOPELESS CASE.

PSALM 88:1–4 (MSG)

D ear friend:

Today you looked as though you have been "camping on the edge of hell." Perhaps the news you received has caused you to feel as though *you* have been "written off as a lost cause, one more statistic, a hopeless case." I cannot know exactly how you feel, but I have felt "written off" before, and I know how painful hopelessness can be.

I suppose the journey through "the valley of the shadow of death" (Ps. 23:4) feels like "the edge of hell." It is important for you to realize, though, that you are only on "the *edge* of hell," not in it. The psalmist was able to make it through his living hell because God did not abandon him. I believe that you, too, will experience, in very mysterious ways, the love of God in the midst of your agony and pain. I believe that angels are present with you, both literally and figuratively. I believe that God is for you and not against you and that even as there is great joy in heaven when a sinner repents, there are also prayers offered and tears shed by the heavenly hosts when God's people suffer.

You are not alone. I love you and will continue to pray for you today. For reasons known only to God, there are those camped on the edge of hell who are allowed to again find rest and water in green pastures. May God's rest be yours today.

Lord, my friend is suffering unbearably today. He is devastated and hurting. Bring comfort and hope to him and to all those who suffer today. In Jesus' name I pray. Amen.

CHAPTER FIVE

God Neither Slumbers nor Sleeps

❖

FOR HE GRANTS SLEEP TO THOSE HE LOVES.

PSALM 127:2

Dear friend:
I stopped by to see you today, but you looked as though you were asleep. I know how hard sleep is to come by around here, so I didn't have the heart to softly call your name to see if you might be awake. I hope you did sleep— deeply and soundly. I did stay a few moments though. And I prayed for you.

As I prayed, the IV machine *ka-lugged* repeatedly. It was hard to concentrate, and I was again reminded that my world and yours are very different places. I have some control in my life. In a moment I will walk out of the room and the noise will cease. You, however, must feel as though you have no power at all. People come and go as they please, waking you up or not, depending upon their workloads.

Happily, you don't need to be awake for my prayers to help you, because as the psalmist reminds us, God "will neither slumber nor sleep" (Ps. 121:4).

As I was leaving, I noticed that you hadn't eaten your lunch and was reminded that chemotherapy often takes away the desire and joy of eating. I prayed that you would eat anyway, because malnutrition causes more deaths than cancer. This one was an "eyes-open" prayer as I walked away. "God," I asked, "please give her the desire to eat, even though it may not taste very good."

I'll check on you tomorrow.

God, how good it is to know that You continually watch over us. Accept our love and gratitude for the little things that we often take for granted, such as appetite and the ability to sleep. Thank You for sleep for my friend today. I'll think of it as a sign of Your love for her. In Jesus' name I pray. Amen.

CHAPTER SIX

Freedom from Negativity

---❖---

DEAR FRIEND, I PRAY THAT YOU MAY ENJOY GOOD HEALTH
AND THAT ALL MAY GO WELL WITH YOU, EVEN AS YOUR
SOUL IS GETTING ALONG WELL.

3 JOHN 2

Dear friend:

Some people wonder whether God wants them to be well. Do you?

Without getting into an in-depth religious discussion using big theological terms, let me appeal to your common sense. God created you, didn't He? Are you not then valuable? Are you not worthy of love, if for no other reason than that you were created by God, whose very essence is love?

I understand why you might wonder, though. It's the pain and suffering, isn't it? It's the nausea. It's the feeling of powerlessness. It is, if you are honest, perhaps a tinge of anger and frustration about the whole situation and the impact that cancer is having not only on your life but also on the lives of your loved ones. I understand. Anger and frustration are as understandable as they are predictable. I would be angry and frustrated too.

I cannot move you from anger to gladness or from frustration to bliss. I can't do anything for you now except to remind you of the truth and trust that the truth will set you free from all the negativity you are feeling right now. Consider this: Thousands upon thousands have gone through what you are going through. Many have been considerably sicker or felt worse than you do and have gone on to reclaim wholeness again.

It's going to be all right. Focus on God's unconditional love for you. It will get better. Trust me. Trust God.

Lord of heaven and earth, grant this day the gift of hope to my friend. As You increase his hope, increase his faith and his capacity to love You, even in spite of doubts, fears, and frustration. In Jesus' name, amen.

CHAPTER SEVEN

Forgiveness and Peace

—————— ❖ ——————

GET RID OF ALL BITTERNESS, RAGE AND ANGER, BRAWLING
AND SLANDER, ALONG WITH EVERY FORM OF MALICE.
BE KIND AND COMPASSIONATE TO ONE ANOTHER, FORGIVING
EACH OTHER, JUST AS IN CHRIST GOD FORGAVE YOU.

EPHESIANS 4:31–32

D ear friend:
Not every moment is a teaching moment. As I
enter into conversations with people, often I have
advice to give but don't do so because the timing just doesn't
seem to be right. Job One in ministry is listening. Job Two is
gaining understanding. Job Three, if the timing is right, is
sharing thoughts and perspectives. Often, the situation doesn't
leave time for Job Three.

Perhaps now might be a good time for me to share with you
my thoughts concerning the matters we discussed earlier. This
is what I would have said this afternoon, had the opportunity
presented itself.

As you described your feelings about a family member who
hurt you, it became obvious to me that you have not forgiven

that person. Were you emotionally abused? Yes. Were you neglected? Yes. Was the person emotionally unavailable even though he was physically present? Yes. Yes. Yes.

But that person has been dead now for twenty years. And yet you are as angry today as you were twenty years ago. As a matter of fact, time does not heal. You told me that you have forgiven. I told you that you haven't. To that statement you responded, "How can I forgive when I can't forget?" and the truth slipped out: You have not forgiven the one who hurt you deeply.

Author Mitch Albom, in his book *Tuesdays with Morrie,* explores the theme of forgiveness of others and of self from within the setting of a painful end-of-life lesson for a dying man. As the story goes, Morrie had never forgiven his friend for not coming to see Morrie's wife when she was terminally ill in the hospital. Although his friend later asked for Morrie's forgiveness, explaining that he had shown his own weakness and inability to cope with illness and death, Morrie was not able to forgive him. On his deathbed, Morrie realized the pain and emotional suffering he had carried with him throughout his life because he could not forgive his friend.

There is a misperception that "to forgive is to forget." This isn't true. Forgiveness is a choice. Forgetting isn't. I cannot choose to forget where I was when I learned that President John F. Kennedy had been shot. I was in my sixth-grade class at Ridgeview Elementary School. My teacher told the class the news, and one of the kids in my class cracked a joke shortly after that. It is a memory etched in time along with other unhappy memories.

Painful experiences are indelibly engraved into our minds. Nothing will ever erase them. However, with genuine forgiveness, the memories can be drained of their pain. They will last, but the pain will be gone.

Forgive your family member. Let him rest in peace. You'll never forget the hurtful experience, but the pain will leave you and be replaced by peace and a body that is better able to battle disease. Forgiveness is a choice. Choose to forgive, lest it continue to affect your body, mind, and soul.

Lord, unlike You, we remember the sins of those who have hurt us. We can, however, choose to forgive. Help us to forgive those who have hurt us, even as You have forgiven us for our own transgressions, to the end that we find ourselves at peace with ourselves, with others, and with You. Help my friend to forgive as he has been forgiven. In Jesus' name, amen.

———————❖———————

PICK UP SOME PAPER
AND A PEN. CONNECT SOME DOTS
THROUGH HONEST REFLECTION.

————————————

CHAPTER EIGHT

Connecting the Emotional Dots

---------- ❖ ----------

"THEN YOU WILL KNOW THE TRUTH,
AND THE TRUTH WILL SET YOU FREE."

JOHN 8:32

"'FOR THIS PEOPLE'S HEART HAS BECOME CALLOUSED; THEY
HARDLY HEAR WITH THEIR EARS, AND THEY HAVE CLOSED THEIR
EYES. OTHERWISE THEY MIGHT SEE WITH THEIR EYES, HEAR WITH
THEIR EARS, UNDERSTAND WITH THEIR HEARTS AND TURN, AND I
WOULD HEAL THEM.' BUT BLESSED ARE YOUR EYES BECAUSE THEY
SEE, AND YOUR EARS BECAUSE THEY HEAR."

MATTHEW 13:15–16

Dear friend:

You told me an amazing story about yourself this morning—about how you were fired from your job and that you are convinced that this traumatic experience led to your getting cancer.

It is true that there is a connection between our emotions and our immune system. Emotional traumas can lead to a wide range of chronic diseases, including cancer. However, you are feeling this way because you are still nursing the wounds of your dismissal.

I wonder why people so often choose to hold on to painful experiences. I don't think it is a conscious decision, although it could be. Usually we hang on to these hurtful situations because we have never learned how to get ourselves out of the webs of our pasts.

One of the ways to process our pain is to write about our lives in an honest way. Groucho Marx once said that it is easier to write about others: We can fudge a few details here or there. But when we write about ourselves, if we do not tell the truth we know that we are liars. The truth can set us free, indeed.

Writing about hurtful experiences forces us to have an encounter with *truth*. As we write, we begin to connect the dots of our lives. We begin to see a more coherent picture of our lives and the decisions we made leading to the situations or circumstances that caused us pain. If we really believe that "all things work together for good" (Rom. 8:28 KJV), perhaps some of our anger and pain is because we haven't connected all of the dots.

Here's the way it works: The more dots you connect, the better you will understand how and why you got where you are. The better you understand that, the less stress you will experience. The less stress you experience, the better your body will be able to fight disease.

Pick up some paper and a pen. Connect some dots through honest reflection. Connect not only the positive experiences, but also the negative experiences, even those times when you exercised poor judgment and made wrong decisions.

How many conversions to Christ have come about when people have connected the dot of sinful behavior to the dot of God's love and forgiveness? Connect the dots—all of them—and trust that as you do, you may experience a truth that will set you free.

Father, why is it that life is so painful sometimes? Why is it that we often make life harder than it needs to be? Why do we avoid truth, even though it will set us free from pain and often disease? Give my friend the desire to connect the dots of her life—day by day, one thing leading to another. Help her to understand her past so that her present may be filled with peace. Amen.

I IMMEDIATELY REPLACED THE THOUGHT
OF QUITTING WITH ANOTHER THOUGHT:
I CHOOSE NOT TO QUIT.

CHAPTER NINE

Choosing to Fight

———————◆———————

BROTHERS, I DO NOT CONSIDER MYSELF YET TO HAVE TAKEN HOLD
OF IT. BUT ONE THING I DO: FORGETTING WHAT IS BEHIND AND
STRAINING TOWARD WHAT IS AHEAD, I PRESS ON TOWARD THE
GOAL TO WIN THE PRIZE FOR WHICH GOD HAS CALLED ME
HEAVENWARD IN CHRIST JESUS.

PHILIPPIANS 3:13–14

Dear friend:

I have arthritis in my right knee. It's probably due to high school athletics and a number of years running in 10K races and a few marathons. Several years ago an orthopedic surgeon told me I'd never run again. Further, he said that the next stop for me would be knee replacement when I am around sixty-five. So I gave up running—for a few years at least.

Then I read about a doctor who utilized his faith in Jesus Christ to help him battle his own arthritis. I thought, *Can arthritis be more devastating than cancer? How can I encourage people with cancer to fight against their chronic disease if I so easily give up on my own?* So I began running again. After a two-year layoff, I am back, huffing, puffing, and faithfully determined not to let my infirmity get me down.

My two-and-a-half-mile route has hills and valleys, ups and downs. Two-thirds of the way through today I almost gave up. I almost quit. I didn't see this attitude coming. I didn't begin my morning run with the thought of quitting, but there I was, facing another hill, and I momentarily found myself quitting.

But it was only for a split second. I immediately replaced the thought of quitting with another thought: *I choose not to quit.* And then I began again, up the hill. A feeling of accomplishment came to me, along with thoughts of you.

I know there are times when you want to quit too, when fighting your disease doesn't seem worth the pain, when the hills you face bring random thoughts of giving up. Choose to fight. Decide not to let your disease control you. Keep running. If you fall behind, I'll wait for you. If I fall behind, wait for me.

Lord, we do not start our days with thoughts of quitting. Sometimes they come out of nowhere. Grant that Your presence within my friend will encourage him to run the good race today and every day. In Jesus' name I pray, amen.

CHAPTER TEN

Unnecessary Unhappiness

---◆---

WHEN I WAS IN GREAT NEED, HE SAVED ME.

PSALM 116:6

WHEN JESUS SAW HIM LYING THERE AND LEARNED THAT
HE HAD BEEN IN THIS CONDITION FOR A LONG TIME,
HE ASKED HIM, "DO YOU WANT TO GET WELL?"

JOHN 5:6

D ear friend:
You seemed unhappy today, and I wasn't quite
sure why. What do you want?

I would never say that directly to you because we barely
know each other. I come into your room for a handful of
minutes and then leave. Without knowing you better, I would
never be so straightforward. But the question remains: What do
you want?

Do you want to get well? I once overheard an old Catholic
priest ask this of one of his parishioners who was bedridden
with heart disease. At the time I thought it was pretty abrupt.
Years later, though, I have come to realize how important the

question is and how the answer to this question can and does help the healer (pastor, priest, doctor, or friend) diagnose the condition of the patient's heart—his motivation, his desire, his preferred future.

Many people complain about life's problems, but few actually get around to doing much about them. It is our nature to complain. That is why suggestion boxes don't work: People put complaints into them instead of solutions. Perhaps the reason the invalid stayed by the pool of Bethesda "for a long time" is that he spent his time complaining about his situation instead of doing something about it.

Most of us have never been taught basic problem-solving skills, and because of this, we find ourselves being *unnecessarily unhappy*. When we are unhappy, we need to ask the question, "What do I want in order for the unhappiness to go away?"

Sometimes we come up with good solutions and are able to solve our problems. Often, though, we cannot figure out a better way to do things. If what we want cannot be accomplished, then our anxiety and complaining only serve to frustrate us and those around us. It is then that we have to adjust our expectations to a new reality that will cause our sadness to dissipate.

For example, you may be sad because you are in the hospital. And yet, being in the hospital is exactly the right decision for you, and the treatment you are getting is unarguably the best course of action for your health. In other words, as you think about it, there is no other rational decision that could be made. This new reality makes your situation much easier to bear, doesn't it?

Someone once wisely said that accepting our limitations makes our future limitless. Narrow your expectations. Adjust them to the reality of your situation. Accept your limited options. Improve them if possible. If what you want is unobtainable, your unrealistic expectations will only make you unnecessarily sad—and probably everyone around you too.

So what do you want? Be clear. Communicate it to those who can help you obtain it. If what you want is unobtainable, ask God to help you adjust to a new and more obtainable reality and a happier future.

Lord, surely You want Your children to be happy and whole. Teach my friend how to experience the blessed life You have created her to enjoy. Move her this day beyond complaining to finding solutions to those things that most concern her. Make her wise in her use of her time and energy, and help her learn to change the things she can change and to accept those things that are beyond her control. Amen.

———————◆———————

GOD ALONE HAS NUMBERED OUR DAYS.
ONLY GOD KNOWS HOW LONG WE HAVE
TO LIVE.

———————————————

CHAPTER ELEVEN

Stealers of Hope

———❖———

HOPE DEFERRED MAKES THE HEART SICK.

PROVERBS 13:12

MAN'S DAYS ARE DETERMINED;
YOU HAVE DECREED THE NUMBER OF HIS MONTHS
AND HAVE SET LIMITS HE CANNOT EXCEED.

JOB 14:5

D**ear friend:**
You told me this morning that the doctor said you have only two months to live. I'm sorry. I cannot imagine how devastating it must be to hear those words. Thoughts of dying must fill your mind. Hope must seem to be evaporating like water on a hot sidewalk.

Unfortunately, I hear diagnoses like this frequently. In the Spirituality and Health class I teach, they are a long way from being rare. I ask the patients to tell me the exact words their oncologists used. Often the words are akin to these: "I am sorry to tell you the bad news. There is nothing more we can do for you. I suggest that you return home and try to make yourself as comfortable as possible. If there is a local hospice, I suggest that you call it." The patient's response is often something like, "Does that mean that there is nothing more that can be done? Am I going to die?" The answer is, "Yes, I am afraid so." One patient told me that when she persisted in asking the doctor for alternatives, he angrily threw his pen on the desk and walked out of his office.

During Bible study this past week, I shared a similar story with our group. One man in the group is suffering from Alzheimer's disease. I can't remember him adding anything meaningful to our discussion in three years. His wife brings him, and the two of them listen and enjoy the fellowship, but he has never, to my recollection, said a word.

After I related the story of a doctor who had told his patient that there was no hope, that she ought to go home and get her affairs in order, that she had only a month to live, the elderly gentlemen with Alzheimer's suddenly blurted out, "Tell him to go to hell!" The group was surprised, and we all laughed because the retort, and the language the quiet man used, was so unexpected. And yet, the words he spoke are the very words I was thinking: *Tell him to go to hell.*

Because, you see, God alone has numbered our days. Only He knows how long we have to live. Every week I see people whose medical-care teams had given up on them, and they are still walking around—usually long after the dates their doctors had estimated.

I cannot understand, nor do I excuse, why a doctor would ever make such negative statements to a patient. Although I am not an MD, I have had conversations with doctors and other health-care professionals, and to a person they have all agreed that such statements are hurtful and unprofessional. Sadly, according to one physician friend of mine, some doctors really do believe that they play the role of God. Hope deferred not only makes the heart sick; it contributes to making the rest of the body sick as well.

Wherever there is life, there is hope. I am glad you did not take your doctor's advice to go home, get your affairs in order, and prepare to die. I am glad your will to live has caused you to seek other alternatives. I cannot promise that your life will be measured in years. Perhaps it will be only in months or days. But they are *your* months, days, and years, not your doctor's. Don't let a doctor steal your hope.

And forgive your doctor. Your anger and bitterness may be justified, but he is only human, and humans make mistakes. Write your doctor a letter to express your disappointment. Send it or throw it away, but get the anger out of you. Let it go, because your anger, though justified, will not help you to be victorious. Rather, it will serve as fuel to the chronic disease that you, with God's help, can learn to live with and overcome.

Lord, how could anyone presume to have all the answers to anything? Forgive those who have tried to defer hope for patients such as this friend of mine. You alone have numbered the days of our lives. Thank You for reminding me that where there is life, there is hope. In Jesus' name, amen.

NOW IS NOT THE TIME
TO BE VAIN.

CHAPTER TWELVE

No Time for Vanity

❖

VANITY OF VANITIES, SAITH THE PREACHER,

VANITY OF VANITIES; ALL IS VANITY.

ECCLESIASTES 1:2 (KJV)

Dear friend:

My mother died from breast cancer fifteen years ago. She was a strikingly beautiful woman. Everyone thought so. She found out that she had breast cancer at the age of sixty-seven, and she was gone by sixty-nine.

It is hard for me to understand my mother's fear of losing her hair. Because she didn't want to lose her beautiful appearance, she sought treatment for her cancer only from herbalists. By the time she learned that this form of therapy alone was not going to heal her, it was too late.

Quite simply, she died because she didn't want to lose her hair. Would someone please explain how vanity can overrule common sense? How concern about physical appearance can obscure good judgment? There is bound to be something I am missing.

If I were to take a guess, I'd say her real reason for making the choices she did had more to do with her belief that cancer was a death sentence, that she was doomed anyway, so why not live her remaining days with as much dignity as possible rather than experience the personal degradation of harsh chemotherapy? This makes sense. She was a very sensible, practical person. Quality of life controlled her decision making because *quantity* of life did not seem to be an option.

On the other hand, perhaps I'm rationalizing. Perhaps there was a dark side to my mother that I didn't know, an inescapable sadness that had enveloped her. Perhaps she didn't take the disease seriously enough. Perhaps she believed she could overcome her cancer through alternative therapies alone.

My advice to you? It's the same advice I would have given to my mother if I had known then what I know now. There are two things that I would advise anyone with cancer to do:

First, fight cancer with every form of therapy available. It is a complex, multifaceted disease that, after invading our bodies, must be fought at the physical, emotional, and spiritual levels.

Second, get at least two opinions from different oncology teams. As an insider, I know there are many of ways to diagnose and treat cancer. Never assume that treating cancer is necessarily "one size fits all" or that the medical community is always in total agreement as to its diagnosis and treatment of this mean disease.

It is safe to say that in the United States all cancer treatment hospitals are good, but they are not all the same. Here's what I mean: Once a cancerous tumor is diagnosed, the medical team *and you* have some options. Perhaps surgery will be required, perhaps not. If the tumor is removed, what then? Still more options.

Some hospitals will begin immediately to administer a chemotherapy or radiation protocol that, based upon their experience, is likely to be the most effective. Some hospitals, on the other hand, send samples of the cancerous tissue to a lab, where technicians treat the samples with various chemicals to determine the most effective therapeutic protocol. Why do they do this? Because some forms of cancer, over time, become resistant to certain chemicals much the way our bodies develop resistances to certain antibiotics.

Given the choice, would you rather the experiment be on *you* or on a *tissue sample*? I am sure you would prefer to let a laboratory determine which drug is likely to be the most effective *before* you start chemotherapy instead of learning later that it wasn't working.

All cancer-care centers are good, but there are differences—important differences—among them. Now is not the time to be vain about your hair. It is not time to be vain about getting second opinions, either. You may lose your hair. You may lose a good relationship with your current doctor. Better that than the possible alternative.

In many cases oncologists are in near total agreement as to both the diagnosis and treatment necessary to fight cancer. Nevertheless, if my mother were living, I would have insisted that she get at least two opinions. There is little room for error, and when it comes to my friends and loved ones, I would rather be safe than sorry.

Father, bless my friend today by shining the light of Your love upon her. Chase away whatever darkness might be enveloping her. Give her hope. Give her options. Give her a long and purposeful life. And remove any and all vain thoughts that might diminish either the quantity or quality of the precious life You have given her. In Jesus' name I pray. Amen.

CHAPTER THIRTEEN

Chronic Niceness

❖

Dear friend:

I was reading an article the other day about a new theory that correlates personality type with cancer. It is becoming known as the Type C (for cancer) personality. In my experiences with hundreds of cancer patients, I have observed no single personality type that is likely to cause cancer or to make a person more prone to getting cancer. Cancer attacks people of all kinds of personalities. It is not gender specific and does not limit its devastating effects to the old and weak. Simply put, cancer is not a respecter of people but rather is indiscriminate in wreaking havoc.

However, over the years experts have noticed that certain characteristics do seem to be present in the personalities of many cancer patients.

For example, studies and observations suggest that many people who get cancer are "chronically nice."[2] My own observations suggest that many cancer patients are nice. Many of the cancer patients I see in the halls of the hospital in which I work are some of the nicest people you would want to meet. Nice? Yes. Chronically? Some are and some are not.

The personality trait being observed as chronic niceness is better identified as passivity. By that I mean that some people being treated for cancer are, by nature, passive. They are passive not only in how they battle cancer but also in many other aspects of their lives. When confronted with a difficult situation, they often acquiesce. They are the ones who seek harmony and peace at all costs.

This personality characteristic can work for you or against you. Always being confrontational isn't going to make you many friends. However, there does come a time when being confrontational is necessary, when being aggressive and assertive is highly desirable. When it comes to your life and health, when it comes to getting second and third opinions about your treatment alternatives, being passive is not helpful. Nor is making friends your ultimate goal.

As you face your battle with cancer, you can choose to be passive or aggressive. All I know is that cancer will not give up without a fight. Jesus was not always nice. He didn't always seek peace. Why should you?

Lord, I have always thought that what it meant to be a Christian is to turn the other cheek and to be a peaceful person—at all costs and in all situations. Help me to rethink this attitude today. Help my friend learn when not to be "nice" in fighting her cancer. In Jesus' name I pray. Amen.

CHAPTER FOURTEEN

A "Can-Do" Attitude

---❖---

I CAN DO EVERYTHING THROUGH HIM WHO GIVES ME STRENGTH.

PHILIPPIANS 4:13

Dear friend:

You seemed a little negative today. Our conversation reminded me of another conversation I had recently with someone who was suffering—admittedly—from a little self-pity and a lot of low self-esteem. He related to me how he had lost his job—again. Apparently he has had difficulty sustaining meaningful employment over the years. He went on to relate to me that the latest job, although not all that rewarding, had been a job that he believed he had "fallen into." It had been a gift from God, or so it seemed.

It became apparent that there was a pattern in his life of getting and losing jobs. He admitted that he didn't think very highly of himself. He even admitted that he didn't blame his employer for firing him, because under the circumstances he had consistently underperformed in his tasks.

As gently as I could, I tried to help this man see that what he needed most wasn't another job but to do some internal work on himself. Otherwise he was just as likely to fail at the next job as he had failed in the past.

What this man lacked was a strong belief in himself, a belief that as a Christian he could do all things through Christ who strengthens him. He needed to

- believe that he is loved and important;
- believe that he is cherished and highly valued by God;
- understand that Christianity and low self-esteem are polar opposites and therefore incompatible; and
- realize that to be a Christian means that we are filled with a "can-do" attitude leading, with God's help, to accomplishing things far beyond what we could otherwise do on our own.

Although there are many jobs to have, there is only one life to be lived. Here's a truth to live by: *What you believe is what you become.* The Bible puts it this way: "As [a man] thinketh in his heart, so is he" (Prov. 23:7 KJV). If someone thinks he is a failure, he will fail. If someone thinks that with God's help he can and will succeed, I believe that positive things will happen.

Perhaps I misread your attitude today and these comments aren't helpful. But if not, let this serve as a reminder: God loves you. God is for you, not against you.

Lord, my friend needs to think positively today. Help him, please, to embrace the promise that he can do all things through Christ who strengthens him. In Jesus' name, amen.

CHAPTER FIFTEEN

A Question of Balance

❖

IS THERE NO BALM IN GILEAD?

JEREMIAH 8:22

D ear friend:
I am much better at giving advice to you than taking advice myself. You and I have one thing in common: We both need to regain a balance in our lives.

The word *medicine,* at its root (*med*), means "middle." Medicine, in other words, means to help a person regain a balance that has been lost, to reestablish harmony, to reacquire equilibrium and homeostasis in the body. You are (or were) in the hospital to regain balance. The questions your health-care professionals are faced with are obvious:

- What is causing your body to be "out of balance"?
- What needs to happen to help your body regain normal, healthy function?
- What can medical professionals do to help you?
- What do you need to do to help yourself?

Scientists are only beginning to discover how the mind, body, and soul interrelate. There are reasons why we get sick, and treating the symptoms of disease is only a temporary remedy. To defeat disease, we have to deal with its underlying root causes.

There is more to a person than a physical body. Our spiritual and emotional sides need balance too. My life at times gets out of balance, and I need to be as committed to regaining a balance spiritually and emotionally as you are physically. I am learning that I have to fight for spiritual wholeness in the same way that you are battling physical disease.

The battle, for me, is either won or lost at the beginning of the day. I have learned that if I start my day with Bible study and prayer, I will be better able to face life's problems. If I do not begin on the "right foot," as it were, I am far more prone to lose my balance and fall into a state of disequilibrium.

When I pray, I try not to ask God for anything in particular. Often my prayer time is spent listening to meditative music while focusing upon the cross of Christ. As I focus upon Christ's tragic death, I am reawakened to the depth of His love for me. His love is the most powerful force in the universe. It is a healing, rejuvenating, redemptive love.

As the hymn says, "There is a balm in Gilead to make the sin-sick whole." Jesus Christ is the balm. His love not only heals our sins but also, I believe, heals our diseases and helps us regain balance in our lives.

Lord, we all need balance in our lives—body, mind, and soul. Help my friend this day to fight for balance in every aspect of life, through the One who loves us enough to die for us, Jesus Christ, our Lord. Amen.

CHAPTER SIXTEEN

Living with Cancer

❖

"I TOOK YOU FROM THE ENDS OF THE EARTH,
FROM ITS FARTHEST CORNERS I CALLED YOU.
I SAID, 'YOU ARE MY SERVANT';
I HAVE CHOSEN YOU AND HAVE NOT REJECTED YOU.
SO DO NOT FEAR, FOR I AM WITH YOU;
DO NOT BE DISMAYED, FOR I AM YOUR GOD.
I WILL STRENGTHEN YOU AND HELP YOU;
I WILL UPHOLD YOU WITH MY RIGHTEOUS RIGHT HAND."

ISAIAH 41:9–10

Dear friend:

When you told me, "It's back," of course I knew exactly what you meant. Your words, though, were unnecessary. Your tears announced the bad news before you spoke.

Fighting cancer—again—is one more hurdle in life that must be overcome. Of course it is a race that you do not want to be in. Of course it is a hurdle you would choose to avoid if possible. But we do not have the luxury of choosing our races. We cannot choose to avoid many of life's hurdles. All the money in the world cannot buy us out of facing some of life's problems. You are in a race that, with God's help, you can win. You are facing a hurdle that, with God's help, you can overcome.

Remember that cancer is a chronic disease like high blood pressure and diabetes. It may be that you will need to learn to live with cancer instead of being permanently cured of it. Perhaps being healed is learning to accept the reality that cancer is going to be part of your life for as long as you live. Thus, some people are cured while others are healed. Healing comes when we allow the Holy Spirit to enter into our lives in such a way that we surrender to reality and lose our fear of whatever the future holds.

You've been over a similar hurdle before and were successful. With God's help, you will be able to overcome it again. So my advice is to "fear not" and trust, again, that God's marvelous healing power will meet you at your point of need. Let the words from Isaiah be God's word to you:

"So do not fear, for I am with you;
do not be dismayed, for I am your God.
I will strengthen you and help you;
I will uphold you with my righteous right hand."

Lord, grant a special measure of peace to my friend who is burdened with bad news. By the power of Your Holy Spirit, may she fly over the hurdle before her without breaking stride in order to continue to run the race that You have set before her. In Jesus' name I pray. Amen.

CHAPTER SEVENTEEN

God's Renewing Power

❖

"IF YOU THEN, THOUGH YOU ARE EVIL,
KNOW HOW TO GIVE GOOD GIFTS TO YOUR CHILDREN,
HOW MUCH MORE WILL YOUR FATHER IN HEAVEN GIVE THE HOLY
SPIRIT TO THOSE WHO ASK HIM!"

LUKE 11:13

Dear friend:

If I wasn't myself today, I am sorry, for I have grown weary. I am "bone tired." I don't mean to lay my problems on you, but the truth is that when I am with you and others who are sick, I give all that I have to give. Some days I seem to have more to give than on other days.

Oddly, I didn't realize how tired I had become until I read a few paragraphs from a book in which the author, also highly engaged in a healing ministry, related her near exhaustion—spiritual exhaustion.

Along with several friends, she prayed for renewal. In her prayer, she said, "Lord, we are washed up ... and if You want us to continue to do Your work You will have to give us the power to do it. So now, if we have heard You correctly You have said

'Pray for the Holy [Spirit].' And we do. We don't know what this means or what will happen to us, but whatever happens, it is all right."[3]

They didn't need new spiritual gifts. They didn't need more faith. They needed energy to continue doing the very thing God had created them to do. They needed the power of God manifested in them through His Holy Spirit. God heard and answered their prayer, and they were renewed, reinvigorated, and empowered to continue doing what they felt called to do.

Maybe you are feeling a little bone tired yourself. Perhaps those around you need to do a little renewing as well. Let's seek God's renewing power together, so that we can both continue living and serving our good and gracious God.

Lord, we feel washed up. We pray that You will fill us anew with Your Holy Spirit. We don't know what this means or what will happen to us, but whatever happens, it is all right. In Jesus' name we pray. Amen.

CHAPTER EIGHTEEN

The Gift of Healing

---❖---

NOW TO EACH ONE THE MANIFESTATION OF THE SPIRIT
IS GIVEN FOR THE COMMON GOOD. TO ONE THERE IS GIVEN
THROUGH THE SPIRIT THE MESSAGE OF WISDOM, TO ANOTHER THE
MESSAGE OF KNOWLEDGE BY MEANS OF THE SAME
SPIRIT, TO ANOTHER FAITH BY THE SAME SPIRIT, TO ANOTHER
GIFTS OF HEALING BY THAT ONE SPIRIT.

1 CORINTHIANS 12:7–9

D ear friend:

I believe that I have the gift of healing. Not the gift of miracles, mind you, but the gift of healing. Healing takes place when body, mind, and soul regain a sense of balance. I have the gift of helping people regain their balance, even if that means helping them adjust to the reality that they are not likely to overcome their diseases. I have learned that helping people adjust to that reality brings them peace. By helping to reduce their fear of death, I believe that I help them to live longer and more meaningful lives.

Sharing this belief with you is both a relief and a burden. It is a relief in the sense that I desire to have an authentic relationship with you. We may be around each other for only a short while, but I have learned that one of the things that characterizes Christians is *love*. Love requires intimacy, and intimacy presupposes self-disclosure. After all, how can two people love one another if they never share who they are with one another? The fact that we may not see each other often means that we have very little time to truly get to know each other. I value our friendship, even though it may be for only a short while, so I was vulnerable with you.

Yet sharing that I have the gift of healing is also a burden to me. I can only imagine what that must have sounded like to you. You must be thinking, *If you have the gift of healing, heal me of my cancer right now!* And in light of the miraculous healings that Jesus and His disciples performed, you are justified in your thoughts. God has used me in numerous situations to heal people, some almost instantaneously. Because I have had these kinds of experiences, I feel somewhat burdened when people are not healed in such a fashion or time frame. I have learned, however, that much of the healing that God accomplishes through me is more subtle than that— and yet no less mysterious.

Without getting too "scientific," I have learned to think more dynamically about healing. We are complex organisms, we humans. The relationship among our minds, bodies, and spirits is only beginning to be understood. The connection between our emotions and immune function has only recently been validated scientifically. [4]

Here's what I believe: As we place our trust in God's love for us and His desire for us to be well, our stress levels go down. As our stress levels go down, our bodies are better able to fight disease in a number of ways, such as through lower levels of cortisol (a hormone that is released in the body during stressed or agitated states), higher levels of IgA (a cancer-fighting enzyme in mucous membranes), higher levels of CD4 (molecules found on some types of T cells that can help you and your doctor decide whether your treatment is working), and lower levels of Interleuken-6 (a protein made by the body that helps regulate the immune system).

My gift of healing grows out of my belief in God's love. As I pray, and as you trust in God, I believe that God unleashes physical mechanisms in your body to battle disease. The physical mechanisms of healing are initiated through the spiritual trigger of faith—yours and mine.

I do not heal. God heals. I simply believe that as I bring people into the presence of our loving God, healing—the regaining of balance—takes place.

Lord, heal my friend, I pray. Not for my sake or his, but for Your sake. And as we pray, may we place our trust in You and in Your love for the whole world, in general, and for us, in particular. Amen.

———————❖———————

WHEN IT COMES TO CANCER,
"ATTITUDE IS EVERYTHING."

———————————————

CHAPTER NINETEEN

A Mind-set for Miracles

———————◆———————

BUT PAUL SHOOK THE SNAKE OFF INTO THE FIRE

AND SUFFERED NO ILL EFFECTS.

ACTS 28:5

———————————

D ear friend:
In some religious circles it is not politically
correct to talk about God perfoming mircles, much
less expect Him to perform them. Sadly, much of my religious
training has overlooked the fact that Jesus empowered His
disciples with the gift of healing. The Bible is replete with
miraculous healings that the disciples performed.

Take, for example, the time Paul was bitten by a snake.
The Bible says that he "shook [it] off into the fire and
suffered no ill effects." I believe that this actually happened.
Those standing around Paul expected him to swell up and
die, but Paul, evidently, had a different mind-set. The poison
as a life-threatening reality was apparently meaningless to
Paul. He simply shook the snake off into the fire.

What did Paul have that we do not? First, he didn't live in a
culture that places its trust in science. Second, he had an

unshakable trust in God. Third, he had such a strong purpose in living for Christ that he couldn't let himself become side-tracked by anything, not even something as life threatening as a snakebite. Perhaps we can learn something from Paul.

In his foreword to my first book, *A Reason for Hope,* Dr. Harold G. Koenig wrote that when it comes to cancer, "attitude is everything." I am only now beginning to understand fully that our attitudes play a far bigger role in our healing than I ever realized.

I have seen miracles, and I have heard about many, many more. Tumors suddenly disappear. Cancer surprisingly kicks into remission. If it is a miracle you need, believe that a miracle is possible in your life. I've seen too much not to encourage you to believe in the supernatural.

Lord, help us to have an unshakable faith in You and make us aware that we, too, have a purpose for our lives. With Your help, may both our faith and life's purpose help us to shake the snakes of our lives into the fire. If it be Your will, grant my friend a miracle, even as You have granted miracles to others throughout the ages. In Jesus' name we pray. Amen.

CHAPTER TWENTY

An Unsatisfying Answer

❖

ALL OF US HAVE BECOME LIKE ONE WHO IS UNCLEAN,

AND ALL OUR RIGHTEOUS ACTS ARE LIKE FILTHY RAGS;

WE ALL SHRIVEL UP LIKE A LEAF,

AND LIKE THE WIND OUR SINS SWEEP US AWAY.

ISAIAH 64:6

FOR IF, BY THE TRESPASS OF THE ONE MAN,

DEATH REIGNED THROUGH THAT ONE MAN, HOW MUCH MORE

WILL THOSE WHO RECEIVE GOD'S ABUNDANT PROVISION OF GRACE

AND OF THE GIFT OF RIGHTEOUSNESS REIGN IN LIFE THROUGH

THE ONE MAN, JESUS CHRIST.

ROMANS 5:17

Dear friend:
"Why do bad things happen to good people?"
Your question deserves a more complete answer than
I gave you the other day.

The answer I have to offer is gleaned from the Bible, both
the Old and New Testaments. I know that reasonable people
can differ when it comes to reading and interpreting Scripture.

Yet my theological reflection, based upon in-depth Bible study, has led me to a single answer to your heart-wrenching question.

Before I give you an answer, let me prepare you for it by saying this: The answer I have to offer will be unsatisfying. The answer the Bible has to offer will not bring a loved one back from the dead. It will not heal you of your cancer or other chronic disease. It will not cure my arthritis.

The reason, according to the Bible, that we have sickness, disease, murder, and divorce, as well as all the other tragic experiences of humankind, is this: sin.

Why do bad things happen to good people? Sin.

Why do you have cancer? Sin.

The Scriptures teach that God created a perfect world without sin. Initially, in the Garden of Eden, there was no sickness or death. Sin was ushered into the world through Adam's disobedience, and the world has never been the same since.

Unsatisfying, isn't it? We want a more identifiable cause in order to inaugurate a more lasting cure.

Sin is as nebulous as the answer is unsatisfying. Did your personal sin contribute to your disease? Well, if you smoked cigarettes for years and got lung cancer, then yes, perhaps the choices you made contributed to your disease. But it may be that your disease has nothing to do with anything you have done. It is merely a consequence of living in a broken world, a consequence that everyone experiences in one way or another. Children, for example, often get sick through no fault of their own.

As members of the human race, this is the sad reality: None of us is immune from sickness and disease. We live in a broken world. In a sense, the whole world is disease ridden because of it. Tragedy and disease are all around us. Yet we are not left to live in despair. There is hope because God, in Jesus Christ, has defeated sin. We cannot avoid tragedy or sickness, because we live in a world infected with sin, but we can overcome it and its effects by placing our faith in Jesus Christ and our trust in God's love to conquer sin—as well as its effects.

Father, to the extent that I am part of this sinful, broken world, forgive me for things I have done that have contributed to the world's problems. Let Your forgiving, healing love shine upon me and through me, through Jesus Christ, our Lord. Amen.

---❖---

CHRISTIANS HAVE EVERY REASON
TO THINK OPTIMISTICALLY.

Positive Thinking

Dear friend:

The other day you told me that you are an atheist. When I asked you to tell me what you believe, you said that you couldn't go so far as to say that there isn't a supreme being, but that for all intents and purposes, for you, God doesn't exist.

You are not alone. You are a member of the world's largest *disorganized* religion, that of *agnosticism*. The word *agnostic* comes from the Greek word *agnostos,* which means "unknown." Agnostics believe that there may be a God who is unknown and unnamed.

Further, there are many in this country who would name Jesus as God but who do not truly know Him. They are nominal

Christians—Christians in name only and agnostic in their religious practices.

What can be done for you? You can mirror the practices of faithful Christians, and as you do, you quite likely will experience positive results, including, perhaps, healing. Think positively.

Christians' "positive thinking" is not something that we manufacture on our own. Nor do we decide to think positively because there may be a positive health benefit. We think positively because we believe that God loves us and wants us to be well. He did not create disease. Through faith in Him, our hope is that we will be able to overcome or learn to live with disease.

Further, we believe that it is human nature to think negatively. We are all prone to become depressed and lose hope. But Christians have every reason to think optimistically. The Scriptures tell stories of healings that undergird our optimism and instruct us how to overcome our diseases. Even from a cursory reading of the New Testament, it is clear that healing is a distinct possibility, if not a likelihood. We believe that if God can raise His Son, Jesus, from the dead, He can and will heal us of our diseases. It may sound far fetched, but that's what we believe and what serves as the source of our optimism.

My advice to you is this: Think positively. God loves you. The extent of His love for you has been revealed through Jesus Christ.

God, I know You are there somewhere. Help my friend to think positively and optimistically about his future with or without cancer. And, God, help him also to believe that Jesus is Your Son. Amen.

CHAPTER TWENTY-TWO

The Inevitability of Pain

---◆---

MY BONES SUFFER MORTAL AGONY
AS MY FOES TAUNT ME,
SAYING TO ME ALL DAY LONG,
"WHERE IS YOUR GOD?"

PSALM 42:10

FOR JUST AS THE SUFFERINGS OF CHRIST
FLOW OVER INTO OUR LIVES, SO ALSO THROUGH
CHRIST OUR COMFORT OVERFLOWS.

2 CORINTHIANS 1:5

Dear friend:
    Just when I think I have some people figured out, I find myself being caught off guard by the depth of their faith in Jesus. How you surprised me this morning! From the outside, you appear to be quiet and cheerful, but on the inside there is such a deep well of faith. Today, as so often is the case, I found myself being ministered to by those God has called me to serve and comfort. Thank you for opening up your

heart and soul to me this morning as we discussed advice you would offer to people with cancer.

When you said, "Focus on Christ's suffering. No one is exempt from pain," I thought to myself, *This is a woman who has faith, not opinions. She's not a seeker but someone whose life overflows with hope and trust, not only when times are good and her body is healthy but also during times of intense suffering.* My, what faith you have!

Right now I have my health, and my life is otherwise pretty good. But that will not always be the case. When the day of my suffering comes, I will remember you and your beautiful cherub face, delightful smile, bald head, and red bandana. I'll remember your faith. I'll also remember your advice: "Focus on Christ's suffering. No one is exempt from pain."

Father, pain and suffering cannot always be avoided. I thank You for my friend's remarkable faith. Grant that when pain comes, she may be faithful to the God who also is well acquainted with suffering and pain. As we consider Christ's suffering, may I always remember its purpose in His life: to die for us. In our suffering, may we live for Him. Amen.

CHAPTER TWENTY-THREE

The Patient as Teacher

❖

AND THE LORD'S SERVANT MUST NOT QUARREL; INSTEAD, HE MUST
BE KIND TO EVERYONE, ABLE TO TEACH, NOT RESENTFUL.

2 TIMOTHY 2:24

Dear friend:

I heard in your voice this morning some frustration about how your family is coping with your disease. Someone once said that a person doesn't get cancer—the whole family does. In a way, it is true. Here's what you need to know: Your family does not know what to do for you or how to do it. They do not know how you feel or what you want them to do. You need to teach them.

I know that the last thing you want to do is teach others while you are learning to cope with your own situation, but the truth, whether you like it or not, is that one of your roles as a cancer patient is also "cancer teacher."

Assuming that your family members want to help you, they need to know that having cancer is a very private experience and that there is a way you would like to be treated and cared for. For example, someone told me the other day that she doesn't want any visitors at all. And if people do come to visit, she would like them to stay for only a few minutes. Your family members need to understand—be taught—that you are the one who is in charge of determining your own needs. They need you to teach them how they can help you get your needs met.

You need to be in charge of *your* life. You need to make decisions with respect to *your* health care. You need to tell your family the most effective and helpful way that, together, you can overcome *your* illness.

You probably don't feel like teaching anyone about anything right now. I understand. Just don't assume that your loved ones know all of your needs.

Lord, my friend is tired. His life doesn't seem to be his own, and here he is learning that it is not enough to be sick, but he has to teach others how to meet his needs. Help him, Lord Jesus, to teach those who want to help, so they will know how to help him best. Amen.

CHAPTER TWENTY-FOUR

The Spirit of Hope

❖

"FOR I KNOW THE PLANS I HAVE FOR YOU,"
DECLARES THE LORD, "PLANS TO PROSPER YOU AND
NOT TO HARM YOU, PLANS TO GIVE YOU HOPE AND A FUTURE.
THEN YOU WILL CALL UPON ME AND COME AND PRAY TO ME, AND I
WILL LISTEN TO YOU. YOU WILL SEEK ME AND
FIND ME WHEN YOU SEEK ME WITH ALL YOUR HEART."

JEREMIAH 29:11–13

Dear friend:

Do you remember the story of Pandora's box? Pandora, according to Greek mythology, was a beautiful woman who was endowed with every gift of skill. The gods made her "all gifted." After placing all of these gifts in a box, they sent her to earth with the command never to look in the box, for in it they had stored the best and worst things they could give to her.

As the story is told, Pandora's curiosity overcame her, and she opened the box, unleashing upon the world a black, stinking cloud of dreadful evils like pestilence, sickness, suffering, hatred, jealousy, and greed. She tried to put the lid back on, but it was too late. From then on, life for humankind was to be difficult. There remained only one thing in the box: the spirit of hope.

Although the Bible gives a different explanation of the reason for suffering in the world, everyone, including the ancient Greeks, knows that life is often difficult. As Christians, we too have a spirit of hope. It is not based upon the power of positive thinking. Our future does not depend upon the capricious whims of an impersonal god, but upon our belief that God cares for each of us and has a plan for our lives.

Your future, and ultimately your hope and mine, is in the nail-pierced hands of Jesus. He has proved trustworthy in the past. May we find comfort in His love today as well as trust that He will also be with us tomorrow, whatever tomorrow may bring.

Lord, sometimes it feels that all my friend has left is his hope for a better tomorrow. Help him to know that his future is certain and that Your plan for his life is for him to prosper. In Jesus' name, amen.

CHAPTER TWENTY-FIVE

The Importance of Hope

---❖---

SUSTAIN ME ACCORDING TO YOUR PROMISE, AND I WILL LIVE;

DO NOT LET MY HOPES BE DASHED.

PSALM 119:116

Dear friend:

I speak often to you about hope because, as everyone knows, hopelessness leads to depression and beyond. The psalmist understood the importance of hope as he pled with God to "not let [his] hopes be dashed."

I believe that when a person loses hope, the body's command center—wherever that is and however it is defined—relays hopelessness to the immune system, which, in turn, causes it to begin to underfunction until such time as the disease overwhelms the defense mechanism and the future is death. It is important to maintain a sense of hopefulness by being reasonably optimistic about the future.

In the Scripture passage quoted above, it would seem that God makes a promise to sustain us, a promise that leads to life and living. Have you ever thought about God's promises to you as a Christian? What promises are there upon which we can depend and upon which we can base our hope?

The psalmist reflected the theology of the Old Covenant, from which grew his understanding of God's promises and subsequent hope, when he wrote:

> But from everlasting to everlasting
> the LORD's love is with those who fear him,
> and his righteousness with their children's children—
> with those who keep his covenant
> and remember to obey his precepts.
>
> Psalm 103:17–18

Here we see that the Lord's love was believed to be with those who continued to be perfectly obedient to His commands. The psalmist's hope, therefore, was ultimately connected to his actions. Presumably, if he were unfaithful, there would appear to be little hope for his recovery.

Christians, on the other hand, can find peace and comfort in knowing that perfect obedience is not a precondition to receiving God's love. Our hope is based upon God's unconditional love for us and not upon any level of moral perfection we might reach. Jesus healed those who needed healing, regardless of whether they were sinners and morally bankrupt. He can heal you too. As you place your trust in God's love, your hope will be both strengthened and renewed.

> He welcomed them and spoke to them about the
> kingdom of God, and healed those who needed healing.
>
> LUKE 9:11

Lord, help my friend to be reasonably optimistic about her future, not because she is always good, deserving, and faithful, but because of Your love for a broken world—a love that heals those who need healing. As long as Your nature is love, O God, we know we have hope. Thank You for Your love for my friend. In Jesus' name, amen.

———————❖———————

As you embrace your suffering
as part of the healing process, the
pain will begin to dissipate.

———————————————

CHAPTER TWENTY-SIX

The Greatest of These Is Hope

❖

AND NOW THESE THREE REMAIN: FAITH, HOPE AND LOVE.
BUT THE GREATEST OF THESE IS LOVE.

1 CORINTHIANS 13:13

Dear friend:

Someone once pointed out that faith seems to answer the *need for spiritual meaning.* Love, on the other hand, relates to the human *need to relate to God, self, and others.* Hope, it is said, reflects the human *motivational need to find meaning and purpose in the future.* The Bible points to hope as a motivator of human effort. For example,

For the grace of God that brings salvation has appeared to all men. It teaches us to say "No" to ungodliness and worldly passions, and to live self-controlled, upright and godly lives in this present age, *while we wait for the blessed hope—the glorious appearing of our great God and Savior, Jesus Christ,* who gave himself for us to redeem us from all wickedness and to purify for himself a people that are his very own, eager to do what is good.

TITUS 2:11–14

In this case, our hope is in a future that includes being forever with Jesus Christ. As Christians, then, we are motivated to live self-controlled lives, eager to do what is good in the knowledge that we will be held accountable to Him for the things we do in the flesh (see 2 Cor. 5:10).

Here and now, though, your immediate future is not heaven. Your immediate future is lying in a bed or sitting in a chair in anticipation of going home. To become well, you may face a future of suffering: radiation, chemotherapy, hair loss, vomiting, sleeplessness, and poor appetite. Some people choose to avoid this suffering in the hope that God will either heal them or take them to heaven quickly and gently. All I can tell you is that Jesus taught us that to fulfill God's plan for His life, He had to suffer. The future God has for you, and the only hope for wellness that you may have, may very well include suffering.

May I encourage you to embrace your suffering as part of God's plan for your life—not as something to be avoided at all costs, but as something to be accepted as part of *your* journey of faith. Here is what you will experience: As you embrace your suffering as part of the healing process, the pain will begin to dissipate. Your body will produce neurochemicals such as endorphins, which, it is said, mimic morphine. By looking at your pain more positively, you will feel better, and your hope for healing and wellness will be restored.

Faith is essential. Love is critical. Right now, for you, "the greatest of these" may be hope: a better future realized through accepting pain as a necessary part of the process of healing.

Lord, at a time like this, when my friend is feeling so sick, give him permission to believe, if but for a moment, that the "greatest of these is hope," because he wants to live and continue to serve Your purposes of love for the world. He needs hope for a better tomorrow, O God. As he suffers today, help him see his pain as a needful and good part of the process of accomplishing Your purpose and will for his life. In Jesus' name I pray. Amen.

———————❖———————

RESIST THE TEMPTATION TO BLAME ANYONE
FOR YOUR CONDITION — NOT YOU,
YOUR FAMILY, OR GOD.

———————————

CHAPTER TWENTY-SEVEN

The Source of Hope

---❖---

PAUL, AN APOSTLE OF CHRIST JESUS BY THE COMMAND OF GOD
OUR SAVIOR AND OF CHRIST JESUS OUR HOPE ...

1 TIMOTHY 1:1

Dear friend:

After we prayed the other day, you gripped my hand as though you never wanted me to leave. I was glad to be there for you and wish I could have stayed with you longer.

It reminded me that there is a fear common to many cancer patients, and that is the fear of leaving the hospital following the conclusion of their treatments. Of course, many are happy to return home, but some, as they leave the hospital and their medical teams, are afraid that they will not be able to survive without them. They worry that they are being unplugged from their lifelines, their sources of hope.

As you leave the hospital, remember that I am not the source of your hope. Your future is not in the hands of the doctors and nurses at the hospital. Your future, and therefore your hope, is in the hands of "Christ Jesus our hope."

My advice to you is not my own, but rather the sage advice of Peggy, another friend and cancer fighter who taught me the importance of doing these things:

1. Cultivate a sense of spirituality, as it is sometimes the only thing that keeps you going.

2. Contemplate Christ's suffering, and remember that no one is exempt from pain and suffering.

3. Resist the temptation to blame anyone for your condition—not you, your family, or God. Now is the time to heal, and blaming anyone for your lack of physical well-being only creates stress for you, which can inhibit your immune system from fully fighting your disease.

4. Set an example for your loved ones to follow and thus teach your family how to respond to your cancer. They do not know how best to help you. You need to teach them.

5. Prepare both ways—for life and living as well as for death and dying.

When I asked Peggy how she has prepared for leaving this life, she said, "Mike, I *know where I am going,* and when I go I do not want to have any regrets or leave any unfinished business."

And so, as you leave to go home, take with you the love of those of us who have served you at the hospital, and take Peggy's advice as well. We are not the source of your hope. We will be here, should you need us again. But be calm and faithful. If you need to talk with me, drop me a line.

Lord, as my friend leaves the hospital, grant that she might know that You are with her always. Help her to live without regret and to finish whatever unfinished business there might be in her life, so that she can focus fully on living the rest of her life, whether measured in days, weeks, months, or years, for You. In Jesus' name I pray. Amen.

———————— ❖ ————————

PAIN IS PART OF LIFE—
WOVEN INTO THE FABRIC OF OUR REALITY,
AND DURING THOSE TIMES GOD REVEALS
HIMSELF TO US IN POWERFUL WAYS.

————————————————

CHAPTER TWENTY-EIGHT

The Best Thing

---❖---

WE DON'T WANT YOU IN THE DARK, FRIENDS, ABOUT HOW HARD IT
WAS WHEN ALL THIS CAME DOWN ON US IN ASIA PROVINCE. IT WAS
SO BAD WE DIDN'T THINK WE WERE GOING TO MAKE IT. WE FELT
LIKE WE'D BEEN SENT TO DEATH ROW, THAT IT WAS ALL OVER FOR
US. AS IT TURNED OUT, IT WAS THE BEST THING THAT COULD HAVE
HAPPENED. INSTEAD OF TRUSTING IN OUR OWN STRENGTH OR WITS
TO GET OUT OF IT, WE WERE FORCED TO TRUST GOD TOTALLY—
NOT A BAD IDEA SINCE HE'S THE GOD WHO RAISES THE DEAD! AND
HE DID IT, RESCUED US FROM CERTAIN DOOM. AND HE'LL DO IT
AGAIN, RESCUING US AS MANY TIMES AS WE NEED RESCUING. YOU
AND YOUR PRAYERS ARE PART OF THE RESCUE OPERATION
—I DON'T WANT YOU IN THE DARK ABOUT THAT EITHER.

2 CORINTHIANS 1:8–11 (MSG)

D ear friend:
  "As it turned out, it was the best thing that could
  have happened." Here we find the apostle Paul
having been face-to-face with death and suffering beyond all
belief. Yet he considered that the spiritual insight he received
from God during his horrific experience was "the best thing

that could have happened [to him]." As I have reminded you repeatedly, pain is part of life—woven into the fabric of our reality, and during those times God reveals Himself to us in powerful ways. This is what Paul was talking about.

My right hand was hit by a boat propeller when I was a student at the University of Texas. Needless to say, the wound was severe. While I was bleeding and before the ambulance arrived, I had a near-death experience. My soul slipped out of my body, and I can still vividly remember looking down at the men putting a tourniquet on my very damaged arm in an attempt to control the flow of blood.

Obviously, I didn't die, but I did learn a spiritual lesson: there is an afterlife. I learned firsthand that there is more to us than our flesh and blood: we have souls.

I wasn't a Christian at the time. In fact, it was nearly ten years before I fully surrendered my life to Jesus Christ, but that tragedy began my quest toward living a fuller, more meaningful life. I now knew that life goes on after we leave this world. That experience, more than any other, changed me from being a worldly nonbeliever to knowing that my essence as a person is spiritual, not physical. I was a short step away from accepting all that the Christian faith teaches about human nature and eternal destiny.

Was it painful? Yes. Tragic? Of course. But I wouldn't trade that horrific experience for anything in the world. "As it turned out, it was the best thing that could have happened."

Lord, help us to embrace our pain and suffering by putting it into a proper perspective. This day, grant Your help so that my friend may see his cancer in a different light, but above all else, use his suffering as an opportunity for him to know You better. In Jesus' name I pray. Amen.

CHAPTER TWENTY-NINE

The Lessons of Suffering

---❖---

So Satan went out from the presence of the Lord and afflicted Job with painful sores from the soles of his feet to the top of his head. Then Job took a piece of broken pottery and scraped himself with it as he sat among the ashes. His wife said to him, "Are you still holding on to your integrity? Curse God and die!" He replied, "You are talking like a foolish woman. Shall we accept good from God, and not trouble?" In all this, Job did not sin in what he said.

JOB 2:7–10

D ear friend:
Suffering is unnatural. God did not create us to suffer but rather to worship and glorify Him. Suffering is of the devil, and no one in history, except for Jesus, has experienced more suffering than Job. Not only did Job physically suffer, but his family and wealth and everything that was important to him were almost completely destroyed.

The book of Job reveals that even though Job faced an enormous foe (Satan), as well as the loss of respect of his wife and friends, he "did not sin in what he said." He refused to "curse God and die." He refused to stop fighting for his life. He refused to stop being faithful and believing in God's love.

Here's what I want you to learn about suffering: It is not God's will for your life, but there are great lessons to be learned as you experience it. As the apostle Paul reminds us:

> We also rejoice in our sufferings, because we know that suffering produces perseverance; perseverance, character; and character, hope. And hope does not disappoint us, because God has poured out his love into our hearts by the Holy Spirit, whom he has given us.
>
> ROMANS 5:3–5

I know you have had enough suffering and you are ready for all of it to end. I lost a dear friend years ago to cancer. Paul's words fell hard on her ears. She had had her fill of "character development." I can only imagine that you feel the same way.

And yet, suffering is a part of life, whether we like it or not. The best we can do is look at it as positively as we can and not let it interfere with our fight for life. Our attitude toward suffering can either be negative, making the suffering we experience meaningless, or positive, as we embrace suffering as part of life and allow it to move us toward greater faithfulness and love for God, who Himself was well acquainted with grief, pain, and suffering. I encourage you to choose life. Fight. Persevere. Hope. And remember Job and his suffering. You are not the first person of faith to suffer, nor will you be the last. Beyond the suffering, I believe, is a better future.

The best part of the book of Job is the ending: "The LORD blessed the latter part of Job's life more than the first" (Job 42:12). Perhaps during the last chapters of our lives we too will see the Lord blessing our lives "more than the first."

Lord, help us find comfort in seeing how You restored Job's life. Give a good ending to our lives in accordance with Your perfect will. In Jesus' name, amen.

—————— ❖ ——————

THE NATURE OF EVIL IS TO CONVINCE THE SICK
THAT THERE IS NO HOPE FOR THEM,
DENYING EVEN THE POSSIBLITY OF A MIRACLE.

—————————————————

CHAPTER THIRTY

Fighting Evil

---❖---

THEN JESUS ARRIVED FROM NAZARETH, ANOINTED BY GOD WITH
THE HOLY SPIRIT, READY FOR ACTION. HE WENT THROUGH THE
COUNTRY HELPING PEOPLE AND HEALING EVERYONE WHO WAS
BEATEN DOWN BY THE DEVIL. HE WAS ABLE TO DO ALL THIS
BECAUSE GOD WAS WITH HIM.

ACTS 10:38 (MSG)

Dear friend:
You asked me about my faith—what I believe about God. You seemed to be interested in why I do what I do with respect to my ministry to cancer patients.

I do what I do because it is a *calling*. God has called me to help heal His broken world. The nature of evil is to destroy life; God is "pro-life." The nature of evil is to woo people away from living the life God created them to live. It tempts them to quit trying to live for God. The nature of evil is to confuse people, to twist and distort facts and subvert truth. The nature of evil is to convince the sick that there is no hope for them, denying even the possibility of a miracle. I see my work with cancer patients as part of the battle against evil in the world.

I believe that cancer, at its core, is spiritual warfare between the authors of good and evil, truth and falsehood, life and death—between the Lord of the universe and the powers and principalities of darkness. Yale physician Sherwin Nuland described cancer cells this way:

> In the community of living tissues, the uncontrolled mob of misfits that is cancer behaves like a gang of perpetually wilding adolescents. They are the juvenile delinquents of cellular society.[5]

This is a good description of evil and the way it runs rampant in the world. And yet, evil was not victorious in the Bible because of the power of love manifested in Jesus Christ. As Jesus' follower, I am committed to seeing that evil is not victorious anywhere—including in your life.

Father, sometimes I feel "beaten down by the Devil." Help me to fight evil in the world. And guard my friend as together we fight the evil that would confuse, weaken, and discourage her were it not for the love and ultimate victory of our Lord Jesus Christ. In Jesus' name I pray. Amen.

Chapter Thirty-one

God's Prevenient Grace

---❖---

Because of his strength will I wait upon thee:
for God is my defence.
The God of my mercy shall prevent me:
God shall let me see my desire upon mine enemies.

Psalm 59:9–10 (kjv)

D ear friend:

If cancer is our enemy, then we have hope that the disease will be defeated because "the God of my mercy shall prevent me."

When we see the word *prevent*, our modern minds translate the word to mean "keep me from doing something." *Prevent*, in our common idiom, means restricting our ability to do or say what we might otherwise do or say.

However, that is not what the word means here. The word *prevent* comes from the Latin word *prevenire*—*pre* (before) and *venire* (to go)—which means "to go before." It is God's promise that, in the fight against evil and disease, we can be assured that not only is God with us, but He is also going before us to ensure that our enemies will be defeated.

God goes before us. Today you will receive treatments that God long ago worked diligently in the minds of biochemists and other health-care professionals to create. Everything good we experience today is the result of God's handiwork—yesterday's busy hands bring us hope for today.

Why am I hopeful? Why should you be hopeful? Because of God's prevenient grace. *The God of mercy shall go before you.*

Merciful God, thank You for all You have done and are doing to help my friend be victorious over all of her enemies—fear, anger, an unforgiving attitude, and doubts, as well as the Evil One, who has come to kill and destroy all life. Help her to remember that every good thing we experience today is the result of what You did for us yesterday. Thank You, Lord Jesus. Amen.

CHAPTER THIRTY-TWO

The Comfort of Scripture

"ARE NOT TWO SPARROWS SOLD FOR A PENNY?
YET NOT ONE OF THEM WILL FALL TO THE GROUND APART
FROM THE WILL OF YOUR FATHER. AND EVEN THE VERY HAIRS
OF YOUR HEAD ARE ALL NUMBERED. SO DON'T BE AFRAID;
YOU ARE WORTH MORE THAN MANY SPARROWS."

MATTHEW 10:29–31

D ear friend:
In my ministry I have noticed that many people who call themselves Christians, when faced with trials and tribulations or serious disease and pain, appear to place little value on their faith in Christ. They needlessly suffer without spiritual comfort. Why do you think that is? Why does their faith seem to evaporate?

My observation is that they often lack the ability to recall biblical passages that God has given to comfort and sustain them. The Word has not been sown permanently into their hearts and minds for the times when tragedy strikes and their lives are threatened. In the heat of the battle, they lack spiritual resources to draw upon for comfort. As Jesus predicted:

"The one who received the seed that fell among the thorns is the man who hears the word, *but the worries of this life* and the deceitfulness of wealth choke it, making it unfruitful."

MATTHEW 13:22

I am not saying that you are like "the one who received the seed that fell among the thorns." I am not suggesting that your life has not borne fruit for the kingdom. The truth I am pointing to is that some people have not taken the Word deeply enough into their hearts and minds, and when the "worries of this life" present themselves, the faith that God has given to them is unhelpful. It does not bear the fruit of fearlessness, comfort, calm, and the assurance of God's love for us. These people forget that God can, and does, help us overcome whatever is threatening us.

Perhaps you might use this time of your life to ponder the Scriptures with a renewed sense of enthusiasm and purpose. They truly are a life source for us all. Remember,

Every part of Scripture is God-breathed and useful one way or another—showing us truth, exposing our rebellion, correcting our mistakes, training us to live God's way.

2 TIMOTHY 3:16 (MSG)

Remember this as well: *You are worth more than many sparrows, so don't be afraid.*

Lord, we have all made more mistakes than we can count, and not meditating upon Your Word just adds to the list. Help my friend to read Your Word more and ponder the glorious riches of truth that are likely to be as close as the drawer next to his bed. In Jesus' name I pray. Amen.

---❖---

DO YOU THINK IT IS POSSIBLE THAT THERE STILL
ARE PEOPLE WHO HAVE THE GIFT OF HEALING?

CHAPTER THIRTY-THREE

Suspicion of the Gift of Healing

AND IN THE CHURCH GOD HAS APPOINTED FIRST OF ALL APOS-
TLES, SECOND PROPHETS, THIRD TEACHERS, THEN WORKERS OF
MIRACLES, ALSO THOSE HAVING GIFTS OF HEALING, THOSE ABLE
TO HELP OTHERS, THOSE WITH GIFTS OF ADMINISTRATION, AND
THOSE SPEAKING IN DIFFERENT KINDS OF TONGUES.

1 CORINTHIANS 12:28

Dear friend:

How do you feel about asking people to pray for you to be healed from cancer? Do you think it is possible that there still are people who have the gift of healing?

It is sad to say that many religious traditions, including my own mainline denomination, are very suspicious of people who claim to have the gift of healing or any other extraordinary gift. These doubters are called "cessationists" because they believe that this and other gifts ceased to exist on earth after the apostles died.

However, I have seen too many healings and experienced too many miracles to believe that God's Spirit has ceased His miraculous works. I believe that God's Spirit is just as actively

101

involved in and through His church today as He was in the days of old. God has not removed His transforming and life-giving power from the church's arsenal of spiritual weapons.

The problem, as I see it, isn't that God has removed His healing, comforting Spirit from the earth. The problem is that we have stopped believing in Him. We've stopped asking for the extraordinary because we feel foolish.

I once had a pastor tell me that I should be "a fool for Christ, but not a damn fool." At the time I thought this was good advice, but years later I have begun to question the wisdom behind the statement. From the pastor's perspective, I guess being "a damn fool" for Christ meant doing things that would cause others to question one's integrity, things that appear crazy or unusual.

I have learned that if that were the standard Jesus used (i.e., if He refrained from doing things that other people think are abnormal), the blind would have never gained their sight, the lepers would have remained sick and separated from society, the paralytic would never have walked, and I would remain hopelessly dead in my sins.

As crazy as it might sound to you, ask for prayers for healing. Perhaps your pastor, chaplain, or doctor has the gift of healing and does not know it because he hasn't tried. Perhaps he is afraid of looking like "a damn fool." I used to feel that way too, but I've learned that there are too many sick people around for me to be overly concerned about what other people may think.

Trust in God. Ask Him for healing.

Lord, help my friend to leave her comfort zone and ask for the healing that You could give—and would give—if she earnestly sought it. Help her to stop caring about what other people think as she seeks help in ways and from people others may think are unusual. In Jesus' name, amen.

———————❖———————

GOOD ANGER IS THE GOD-GIVEN EMOTION
THAT PRECEDES POSITIVE CHANGES.

———————————————

CHAPTER THIRTY-FOUR

Good and Angry

GO AHEAD AND BE ANGRY. YOU DO WELL TO BE ANGRY—
BUT DON'T USE YOUR ANGER AS FUEL FOR REVENGE. AND DON'T
STAY ANGRY. DON'T GO TO BED ANGRY.

EPHESIANS 4:26 (MSG)

Dear friend:

Most Christians I know believe that it is wrong to express their anger at someone. They think that they ought to always "turn the other cheek" and therefore avoid confronting difficult situations and difficult people.

However, *complete passivity* is *not* what the Bible teaches us. Jesus got angry, and the money changers in the temple got the brunt of it one day (see Matt. 21:12). Jesus got mad at Peter once. "Get thee behind me, Satan," He said (Matt. 16:23 KJV). Getting angry is not bad. It is one of many feelings that God has given to us for specific purposes. Good anger is the God-given emotion that precedes positive change. For example, I'm sure you can think of instances in which

- a wrong was righted because someone was angry;
- a sin was tamed because someone was angry;

- an unfairness was made fair or an injustice made just because someone was angry;
- a disease was cured because someone was angry;
- weight was lost because someone was angry; and
- a bad habit was corrected because someone was angry.

Some people need to be taught or given permission or encouraged to express their anger. Do you need permission to get angry?

Others need to control their emotions better. Does that describe you? Often, the words we use when we are angry underscore what we truly believe. Dr. Herbert Benson of Harvard Medical School teaches that "what we believe, we become."[6] If that is true, then we ought to listen to the words we use when we are angry.

Have you ever caught yourself saying, "I'm never going to get rid of this cancer" or "My hair is never going to grow back" or "I always throw up every time I get this chemo treatment"? You have reasons to be angry. You feel powerless over your situation, which is the source of your anger. But it is often the case that our "self-talk" sets us up for failure. Try changing these words to more reasonable and less emotionally charged words, such as "I might be able to get rid of this cancer" or "I sometimes get sick during chemotherapy."

Learning how to deal with anger is hard enough for most of us. Consider not making it any harder on yourself than it already is. You do not know the future. Leave words like *never* and *always* to God. You'll feel better using words like *might* and *maybe*.

Lord, help my friend deal with his anger—to express it posi-tively and to refrain from creating more problems for himself than he already has. Help him to leave his uncertain future in the sure and certain hands of the One who said, "And surely I am with you always, to the very end of the age" (Matt. 28:20). In Jesus' name I pray. Amen.

———————❖———————

LIFE IN THE HOSPITAL CAN BE TOUGH,
AND WE KNOW THAT YOU WILL GET ANGRY
AND FRUSTRATED AND THAT WE WILL, IN
ALL LIKELIHOOD, SEE YOU AT YOUR WORST.

———————————————

CHAPTER THIRTY-FIVE

Mood Swings of Exhaustion

---❖---

DO YOU NOT KNOW?
HAVE YOU NOT HEARD?
THE LORD IS THE EVERLASTING GOD,
THE CREATOR OF THE ENDS OF THE EARTH.
HE WILL NOT GROW TIRED OR WEARY,
AND HIS UNDERSTANDING NO ONE CAN FATHOM.
HE GIVES STRENGTH TO THE WEARY
AND INCREASES THE POWER OF THE WEAK.
EVEN YOUTHS GROW TIRED AND WEARY,
AND YOUNG MEN STUMBLE AND FALL;
BUT THOSE WHO HOPE IN THE LORD
WILL RENEW THEIR STRENGTH.
THEY WILL SOAR ON WINGS LIKE EAGLES;
THEY WILL RUN AND NOT GROW WEARY,
THEY WILL WALK AND NOT BE FAINT.

ISAIAH 40:28–31

Dear friend:

Do you ever have mood swings? One moment you are calm and in control, and the next moment you are irritated beyond belief—almost as if you were two different people?

If you experience these mood swings, it is probably because you are exhausted. When we get bone tired, we lose our ability to stay in control of our emotions. That is when we are most vulnerable, and we are likely to lash out and do or say something we might later regret.

Here is some good news for you: Your doctors and nurses and the rest of your medical team have seen it all before. We know you are exhausted and that you are being pushed and pulled to the point that you hardly ever get a good night's sleep. We even know that sometimes we have to wake you up to give you a sleeping pill! Life in the hospital can be tough, and we know that you will get angry and frustrated and that we will, in all likelihood, see you at your worst.

It's okay. We are professionals. We love and accept you, even when you get testy.

We also know that those who grow tired and weary will stumble and fall, but that hope in the Lord will renew their strength. There will be better days ahead, I assure you.

Lord, thank You for sleep and rest for my friend. Forgive her if she is not herself today, and help her to appreciate the good efforts of her caregivers, who are probably even more tired than she is. In Jesus' name I pray. Amen.

CHAPTER THIRTY-SIX

Ordained to Be a Friend

❖

IF ONE FALLS DOWN,

HIS FRIEND CAN HELP HIM UP.

BUT PITY THE MAN WHO FALLS

AND HAS NO ONE TO HELP HIM UP!

ECCLESIASTES 4:10

Dear friend:

When I was a seminary student, part of my training was in a chaplaincy program called CPE. The goal of the CPE program is to identify interpersonal issues that need to be worked on *before* a person gets into a church ministry instead of afterward.

One of the idiosyncrasies that I discovered in myself was that I was overconfident in my ability to help people. I really believed that if I tried very hard I could make a positive difference. I could help them transform their lives. I suppose the reason I thought this was that God had transformed mine.

I was new to ministry and idealistic too. Then one day I went into the room of a man who was going to die if he didn't get a heart transplant. He refused to have the transplant. I spent time with him and developed a pseudo friendship, but I still couldn't convince him to want to live.

My adviser explained the problem to me this way: "Mike, he hasn't ordained you to be his pastor. His fishing buddy or high school sweetheart might be able to convince him in a minute to have the operation, but until he 'ordains' you to the role of adviser and confidant, he's not going to listen to you."

And so I know my limits with you. I can't make you want to live. You are precious to God, to your family, and to your friends—and life, though not painless, is good. I can't make you get the treatments you need, horrible side effects and all, but there probably is someone out there who could convince you to want to live. Do you have such a friend? Who have you "ordained" to be your confidant and adviser? If such a person exists, please call him or her.

Perhaps you do not have a friend who is there to pick you up when you fall. You have no idea how much I want to be your friend. You cannot imagine how much your chaplains, social service workers, doctors, and nurses want to be your friends as well. Why? Because it is in the context of friendship that truth is best offered and received and healing takes place.

Allowing us to be your friends at this difficult time of your life is the greatest honor you could bestow upon any of us. It would be an honor to help you, to serve you, to love you, for us to trust each other—one friend to another.

Have a friend? Need a friend? All you need to do is ask.

Lord, bring to my friend those people who know him best and love him most. Help him want to live, if not for himself, then for them—and for You. In Jesus' name I pray. Amen.

CHAPTER THIRTY-SEVEN

Miracles of Spontaneous Remission

---❖---

JESUS REACHED OUT HIS HAND AND TOUCHED THE MAN.
"I AM WILLING," HE SAID. "BE CLEAN!"
IMMEDIATELY HE WAS CURED OF HIS LEPROSY.

MATTHEW 8:3

Dear friend:

Most often, when the Lord healed someone, the healing was immediate. The lepers, the blind, the paralytic, and the lame were healed immediately. He even raised His friend Lazarus from the dead *instantaneously.*

On two occasions I have prayed with people who had cancerous tumors on the spine. Both were heading for surgery soon. Both were experiencing debilitating effects caused by the cancer, such as numbness in their legs or stomach problems. Both were healed immediately. The tumors simply disappeared, and the attending surgeons were unable to find them.

I have heard similar stories from others about this phenomenon called "spontaneous remission." Everyone agrees that it is a rare occurrence. Along with me, everyone wonders why it is so rare. As one expert put it:

A spontaneous remission is the disappearance of cancer without any immediate medical cause. As my former employer, Memorial Sloan-Kettering President Lewis Thomas, MD, once said: "The rare but spectacular phenomenon of spontaneous remission of cancer persists in the annals of medicine, totally inexplicable but real, a hypothetical straw to clutch in the search for a cure.... No one doubts the validity of the observation."

The number of patients who experience a spontaneous remission has always been small, and is growing smaller. But it is a fact, and seeing it, or even reading about it, alters one's view of reality. It is like suddenly seeing a UFO appear in the night sky. It shakes your ordinary convictions and demands a profound change in worldview. After all, if Nature can do this, why can't we mortals learn the trick and start to do it ourselves?[7]

Why is the occurrence of spontaneous remission becoming rarer? Is it because we are becoming increasingly skeptical about the existence of God and what His transforming power can do?

I remember entering a Roman Catholic church in south Texas that had a not-so-small room near the sanctuary. It had crutches hanging on the wall, wheelchairs folded up and unused, and many photocopies of letters that people had written to God thanking Him for the healing they had experienced. The room contained evidence of story after story of miraculous happenings. There are probably medical reasons that explain the apparent fact of fewer and fewer spontaneous remissions taking place, but I do wonder if there isn't some mind-body, spirituality-health, or faith-related correlation.

Miracles are not given by God for the purpose of healing us, which of course is what happens. God performs miracles as a sign of His existence, His power, and His love. Miracles create opportunities for God's people to praise Him, which is the reason God created us in the first place. If you are fortunate enough to experience a miracle—and they do happen—dedicate a good portion of your life to sharing that marvelous experience with others, telling them of the great things God has done for you.

Lord, my friend's faith is not as strong as Your love. As You consider her for a miracle, please don't hold her halfhearted devotion against her. Heal her, I pray. And when she is healed, help her tell everyone of the great things You have done for her. In Jesus' name I pray. Amen.

---❖---

EXPERTS TELL US THAT DEPRESSION
AND OTHER CHRONIC EMOTIONAL PROBLEMS
CAN WEAKEN THE IMMUNE SYSTEM'S
EFFECTIVENESS IN COMBATING CANCER.

CHAPTER THIRTY-EIGHT

A Prison of Depression

———————— ❖ ————————

I CAN HARDLY WAIT TO CONTINUE ON MY COURSE.
I DON'T EXPECT TO BE EMBARRASSED IN THE LEAST.
ON THE CONTRARY, EVERYTHING HAPPENING TO ME IN THIS JAIL
ONLY SERVES TO MAKE CHRIST MORE ACCURATELY KNOWN,
REGARDLESS OF WHETHER I LIVE OR DIE.
THEY DIDN'T SHUT ME UP; THEY GAVE ME A PULPIT!

PHILIPPIANS 1:20 (MSG)

———————————————

Dear friend:

As I minister to cancer patients, I am always scanning for a number of things. I look for signals such as hopefulness, a fighting attitude, a willingness to take control of one's own health care, and a level of social support, among others. One huge "red flag" that I look for is depression.

You looked depressed today. I hope I am wrong, that my diagnosis was incorrect. I cannot always know what is going on inside a person, but body language is almost always a trustworthy barometer. We really don't hide our feelings as well as we might think we do, and you seemed sad and depressed today. Am I close?

It is important for you to know that experts tell us that depression and other chronic emotional problems can weaken the immune system's effectiveness in combating cancer. Depression and stress inhibit the production of immune cells, such as lymphocytes, and in the long term it can increase susceptibility to other disease.[8]

If you are depressed, what can you do? Several things. The first, of course, is to recognize it and ask for help from your health-care team. There are counselors and other mental health-care professionals available to help you learn how to better cope with your disease.

Second, it seems to me that our faith ought to play a positive role in our attitudes as well. As I read the New Testament, I see both Jesus and Paul experiencing tremendous stress. Perhaps they occasionally got depressed and sad. Surely the scene of Jesus in the Garden of Gethsemane illustrates His tremendous despair, and yet He was able to continue His journey. He did not allow His sadness to keep Him from doing what God had called Him to do.

Paul, on the other hand, was usually able to "reframe" his situations. He was able to look at difficult situations through a very special lens. He was convinced that God was working in and through all situations, even the otherwise depressing ones, such as being put in jail. Instead of becoming depressed over his fate, he said, "They didn't shut me up; they gave me a pulpit!"

It would be an insult to take your feelings lightly and not be sympathetic. It would be, perhaps, an even bigger insult to let you sink deeper and deeper into despair. It simply is not helpful right now.

You are not behind bars, but if you are not careful, you can build a prison for yourself that may be inescapable. Please talk to someone soon. Call me—collect—if you need me.

Lord, my friend needs Your help to look at life's circumstances differently. Help him turn his bed into a pulpit from which he can proclaim Your life-giving love and mercy. In Jesus' name I pray. Amen.

WITHOUT ANY DOUBT I BELIEVE THAT
FAITHFUL PRAYERS ARE HEARD BY
GOD AND ANSWERED.

CHAPTER THIRTY-NINE

Prayer as Medical Protocol

---◆---

"I TELL YOU THE TRUTH, IF ANYONE SAYS TO THIS MOUNTAIN, 'GO,
THROW YOURSELF INTO THE SEA,' AND DOES NOT DOUBT IN HIS
HEART BUT BELIEVES THAT WHAT HE SAYS WILL HAPPEN,
IT WILL BE DONE FOR HIM. THEREFORE I TELL YOU,
WHATEVER YOU ASK FOR IN PRAYER, BELIEVE THAT YOU HAVE
RECEIVED IT, AND IT WILL BE YOURS."

MARK 11:23–24

Dear friend:

My experience has been that most Christians do not know how to pray for cancer patients. They are not sure what to pray for. They do not know which words to use, nor do they realize how critically important prayer is in the healing process. Therefore they keep their thoughts and prayers to themselves.

I taught a course to some MDs a while back, and several of the doctors wanted to know what words to use as they prayed for their patients. They, like most of us, grope for the right words to speak at the right time.

Jesus may not teach us which words to use, aside from the Lord's Prayer, but He does teach us this quite plainly: "Whatever you ask for in prayer, believe that you have received it, and it will be yours." At one level this seems both ridiculous and hurtful. After all, how can we pray for someone who is critically ill with cancer to be healed of it, especially when we know (or think we know) what the statistics tell us about its morbidity?

In the past, I have been concerned about manipulating patients by appearing to provide false hope. I have been cautious of being too bold, but not anymore. Without any doubt I believe that faithful prayers are heard by God and answered.

The prayer I use regularly grows out of a firm belief that if I pray *in accordance with God's will*, God will answer it. If I pray for *my* will to be done, instead of the Father's, I should not anticipate any positive outcome. My ultimate trust is in God's goodness, in His knowledge of what is best for me and for you, and in His ability to bring it to pass.

God does not want to impose His will upon us. He does not force us into submission. But when we finally do seek His will and promise to submit ourselves to it, good things happen. This is what I believe, and it is based upon seeing God do the most amazingly unexpected things you can imagine. God answers prayers.

When I pray, I use variations of the following prayer. Let it be my prayer for you.

Lord, if it be Your will, please heal my friend. No one, including both of us, wants to live one minute outside of Your will, so if it be Your will, shine Your healing light upon her right now. May her immune system begin now to produce additional natural killer cells, may her cortisol level begin now to go down, may her CD4 level begin now to rise, to the end that her body will regain its strength to fight this mean disease. You tell us that if we ask, we shall receive, and I believe Your promise. I humbly ask for healing, trusting in Your goodness and Your love for all life, including ours. Thank You for Your healing that I believe is taking place. In Jesus' name I pray. Amen.

———————— ❖ ————————

SCIENTISTS NOW KNOW THE HEALTH BENEFITS OF
FORGIVING OTHERS, AND OURSELVES, FOR ANY
HARM THAT HAS BEEN INFLICTED UPON US—
EMOTIONALLY OR PHYSICALLY.

————————————————

CHAPTER FORTY

Be. Do. Have.

❖

DON'T YOU KNOW THAT YOU YOURSELVES ARE
GOD'S TEMPLE AND THAT GOD'S SPIRIT LIVES IN YOU?

1 CORINTHIANS 3:16

D ear friend:

How often do you attend religious services?

Which, if any, denomination or religious tradition are you affiliated with? Are you religiously conservative or liberal?

These are not my questions but the kinds of questions bioscientists are asking hospitalized patients these days to determine if there appears to be any relationship between faith and health or, if you prefer, mind and body.

What they have learned is that people who best cope with and overcome disease are conservative Protestants who regularly attend worship services.[9] What is it about conservative Protestants that appears to make them better candidates for longer, healthier lives?

Perhaps, though not always, they read and study their Bibles more. A thorough reading of the Scriptures teaches themes that we now know have enormously positive impact upon our health.

Forgiveness. Scientists now know the health benefits of forgiving others, and ourselves, for any harm that has been inflicted upon us—emotionally or physically. People who do not forgive as God has forgiven them become sicker more often, and they are not as resilient in their recovery from disease. There is no health benefit in harboring anger. The cross of Jesus Christ is emptied of its meaning apart from forgiveness. Here's the lesson: Holding anger creates stress. Stress negatively affects our immune systems. An underperforming immune system creates an optimum environment for vulnerability to disease.

Respect for our bodies. The Scriptures also teach that one's body is the temple of the Holy Spirit. As such, conservative Protestants—those who believe in the Bible and practice their faith—often take better care of themselves. They smoke less. They drink less. They are less likely to engage in other high-risk behaviors because of their belief in the value of life and the holiness of their physical bodies.

Trust in God. The older I get, the more I am convinced that the biggest lesson God wants us to learn is to trust in Him. Among other needs, He wants us to trust Him for our:

- daily bread (Luke 11:3),
- protection (Ps. 20:7),
- victory over adversaries (Ps. 25:2–3), and
- personal peace (Ps. 125:1; John 14:1).

In fact, after three years of training at Princeton Theological Seminary, the last words I heard on the last day of classes were these: *"When all else fails, trust God."* And while we all know that we should trust God first and foremost, the embarrassing fact is that we tend to look to our own human resources first, then cast our burdens on God after we have exhausted our own efforts. Although we may know better, most of us really do believe that "God helps those who help themselves" (which is *not* in the Bible!) when in reality God helps those who ask for His help. Remember these important words from Jesus:

> "Ask and it will be given to you; seek and you will find; knock and the door will be opened to you. For everyone who asks receives; he who seeks finds; and to him who knocks, the door will be opened."
>
> MATTHEW 7:7–8

Whatever level of trust you now have in God, now is the time for you to trust in Him completely. Envision your life in the palm of His good and merciful hand. Invite Him to do with you whatever pleases Him. As Mary, the mother of Christ, said so faithfully to the angel Gabriel upon learning she was going to give birth to the Messiah—"May it be to me as you have said" (Luke 1:38)—so may you also accept God's perfect plan for your life, however inconvenient, unexpected, or unwanted.

As they trust in God's matchless love and concern, those faithful to Him experience an unparalleled sense of peace. I want this peace for you.

I have lived much of my life believing a simple credo: *Be. Do. Have.* If you want to *be* successful, *do* the things successful people do, and you will *have* the things successful people have. Even if you are not a conservative Protestant, studies show we would all do well to do what they do. Worship regularly. Read the Bible. Talk with God through prayer. Take good care of your body. Forgive those who have hurt you. Trust in God.

Father, let my friend begin his recovery today. Regardless of what he did or didn't do in the past, let him begin again by immersing himself in Your grace. Bathe him in Your grace. Wash him in Your forgiveness. Rinse him with Your love. Help him to begin there today—and to end there as well. In Jesus' name I pray. Amen.

CHAPTER FORTY-ONE

The Unfairness of It All

❖

Dear friend:

You caught me off guard this morning with your tears. Yours eyes welled up, tears flowed uncontrollably, and I wanted so desperately to do or say something to help ease your pain. All I could do was squeeze your hand and offer what I hope was an understanding look.

You said you come from a family of criers, and I believe you. I could see your sister out of the corner of my eye, and she was crying too. If ever there was a passage that I hope is prophetic it is this: "Those who sow in tears / will reap with songs of joy."

When I asked you why you were crying, you said, "I don't know." But, reading between the lines, I sensed that your tears are the tears of someone who is angry and frustrated. They are the tears of someone who feels like she has been treated unfairly.

You mentioned that you felt it was unfair for someone your age, with young children and a long life ahead of you, to get cancer. Unfair? I've talked to you before about the biblical story of Job. He also struggled with issues of "fairness." He said,

> "Mighty God! Far beyond our reach!
> Unsurpassable in power and justice!
> It's unthinkable that he'd treat anyone unfairly."
>
> JOB 37:23 (MSG)

No doubt Job is right. Although the suffering we experience seems and feels unfair, surely God's fairness is something we must presume.

I would like you to dismiss thoughts of unfairness for another reason too. There is a high correlation between our perception of unfairness and our level of anger. In other words, the more unfair something seems, the angrier we get.

Anger can lead to righting a wrong, but in your case, the anger is useless. Your anger cannot cure your cancer, except to the extent that it fortifies your determination to fight the disease. In fact, your belief that life is unfair is creating stress that suffocates your immune system. Imagine your immune system as a water hose. Your anger is like stepping on the hose, thereby inhibiting the flow of life-giving, cancer-curing natural killer cells and other cancer-fighting enzymes throughout your body.

Advice? I don't know, my friend. All I know is that I want you to want to live, and the best way I know to help you live is to encourage you to harness anger to spur you to action in taking on your illness. Then relinquish all anger or thoughts of unfairness to God, and let His unexplainable peace fill your body, mind, and spirit.

Lord, for reasons known only to You, cancer is a part of my friend's life. Help her to let go of her anger and frustration. Replace her tears, I most humbly pray, with songs of joy. In Jesus' name I pray. Amen.

———————————❖———————————

REMEMBER, IT IS *YOUR* LIFE. NOW IS NOT
THE TIME TO WORRY ABOUT HURTING YOUR DOCTOR'S
FEELINGS BY GETTING A SECOND OR THIRD OPINION.

———————————————————

CHAPTER FORTY-TWO

Trust but Verify

---❖---

BE KIND TO ME, GOD—
I'M IN DEEP, DEEP TROUBLE AGAIN.
I'VE CRIED MY EYES OUT;
I FEEL HOLLOW INSIDE.
MY LIFE LEAKS AWAY, GROAN BY GROAN;
MY YEARS FADE OUT IN SIGHS.
MY TROUBLES HAVE WORN ME OUT,
TURNED MY BONES TO POWDER....
BE BRAVE. BE STRONG. DON'T GIVE UP.
EXPECT GOD TO GET HERE SOON.

PSALM 31:9–10, 24 (MSG)

Dear friend:

You asked me what I think about getting a second opinion of your diagnosis. Questions like this are difficult, if for no other reason than that I am a religious professional working in an environment where medical professionals reign supreme.

The first thing I would tell you is that I have not been to medical school. Your health-care professionals are highly trained and highly skilled and probably know more about treating cancer from a medical standpoint than I will ever know. Here is what I want you to know: Your doctors are trustworthy. Trust them. Believe in them and the medical protocol they have established for you. This is a critically important component to your overcoming cancer. Trust, trust, trust.

However, knowing what I know about cancer treatment and the endless information that is available on the subject, my advice also includes this word of caution: *verify.*

Trust but verify.

If I were to develop cancer, I would get two or three opinions before I settled on one doctor or one team of doctors. After the consultations, you may not be any more certain of which one to choose, but at least you will have exercised "due diligence" with respect to investigating your options.

Remember, it is *your* life. Now is not the time to worry about hurting your doctor's feelings by getting a second or third opinion. In light of the situation, your doctor understands how important it is for you to know that all options are being investigated and to select a doctor in whom you have the highest confidence. You need to be able to have profound faith in your doctor's judgment and in her commitment to helping you overcome your disease.

If you have the luxury, trust but verify. If you don't have that luxury, for whatever reason, remember that doctors' credentials have earned them the right to have your trust.

Listen. Learn. Trust. Obey.

Lord, thank You for my friend's doctors. I pray for them. As on most days, they will be busy today, so I ask that in the

busyness of their day You bless them with Your love and guid-
ance as they bring health and healing to their patients. Help
my friend to listen to, learn from, and obey them as well as
You. Help him to be brave, to be strong and not give up. In
Jesus' name I pray. Amen.

IF YOU HAVE FAITH THE SIZE OF A MUSTARD SEED,
YOU CAN MOVE MOUNTAINS.

CHAPTER FORTY-THREE

Size Doesn't Matter

---◆---

GOD'S NOW AT MY SIDE AND I'M NOT AFRAID;

WHO WOULD DARE LAY A HAND ON ME?

GOD'S MY STRONG CHAMPION;

I FLICK OFF MY ENEMIES LIKE FLIES.

FAR BETTER TO TAKE REFUGE IN GOD

THAN TRUST IN PEOPLE.

PSALM 118:6–8 (MSG)

Dear friend:

This morning you compared your faith (or perceived lack of it) with that of someone who you thought was a perfect example of the Christian faith. You lamented that your faith is not as strong as it could or should be, and you wished that you had more of whatever it was you saw in that other person.

Your perception may be right. That person may have more faith than you do. The Bible teaches us that some people have been given the gift of *faith*,[10] which is to say that some people seem to have extraordinary faith. Of course, every believer has *some* faith; it's just that some people are stronger in that area than others.

As a pastor, I am always blessed by the strong faith of many people in my congregation. Sometimes it makes me feel inadequate too. But I have stopped comparing myself to them—my faith to theirs—and have learned to warm my hands by the fire of their faith. I've learned that God sends people into my life to encourage and remind me of His love as well as to hold me accountable to biblical truth.

There is more to know about faith than how much you have or don't have. The most important thing to remember is that however much you have, you have enough to move mountains. Jesus said, "I tell you the truth, if you have faith as small as a mustard seed, you can say to this mountain, 'Move from here to there' and it will move. Nothing will be impossible for you" (Matt. 17:20).

If you have faith the size of a mustard seed, you can move mountains. And if you can move mountains, you can surely "flick off [your] enemies like flies." Flick off the enemy of doubt right now. You have faith. You have all the faith you need to warrant God's love and attention.

Lord, as we look around we so often see people who seem so much more religious than we are. They quote Scripture and share their faith. My friend has faith too, Lord, though today it may be as small as a mustard seed. She has faith in Your love for her and in Your desire for her to become well. Today, in the name of Jesus Christ, I ask that You help her choose to move the mighty mountain of doubt into the sea, to flick it away from her like a fly. And help her commit herself to stop comparing her faith to that of others. Rather, help her to thank You for the faith she does have, just as it is. Thank You. Thank You. Thank You. In Jesus' name I pray. Amen.

―――――――――❖―――――――――

"I HAVE PRAYED FOR HEALING, AND I
HAVE NOT BEEN HEALED. DOESN'T GOD LOVE ME?"

―――――――――――――――――――

CHAPTER FORTY-FOUR

The *Real* Problem

---❖---

BE JOYFUL IN HOPE, PATIENT IN AFFLICTION,

FAITHFUL IN PRAYER.

ROMANS 12:12

Dear friend:
You asked me what I thought about prayer. You wanted to know if it works and how and why it works. As often is the case, I tried to read between the lines in an attempt to discern what was prompting you to ask these deep, probing questions.

I have learned that the *presenting* problem is almost never the *real* problem. For example, in one marriage counseling session, a wife began our conversation by telling me how depressed she was. The reason, predictably, was her husband's behavior, and the entire blame for her sadness fell upon him. This is a common scenario. The *presenting* problem was her husband's behavior, and her initial request was for me to help "fix" her husband.

Upon further exploration, however, we discovered that the real problem wasn't her husband's behavior; it was the enormous amount of time she was spending at the church, which was taking away from important time with her family. She realized that if she changed her behavior, she would alter her husband's as well.

There is almost always a different real problem behind the presenting problem. So my thoughts, conditioned by my clinical training, require me to read between the lines and probe a little more deeply. Why are you asking these questions about prayer? What do you believe about prayer? Do you believe in God's ability to hear and answer prayer?

Here's what may lie behind your question: "I have prayed for healing, and I have not been healed. Doesn't God love me?" Am I close?

A brief answer to your question is this: I always believe that God answers my prayers if I'm praying in accordance with His will. Because I am never 100 percent certain of what God's will is for my life, I place myself before His loving presence in prayer, seeking His will and choosing to surrender myself to whatever may happen. And whether the time God gives me to live will be measured in days, weeks, months, or years, whatever He has ordained for me is sufficient.

I find comfort in the following words. I pray that you do as well.

For you created my inmost being;
you knit me together in my mother's womb.
I praise you because I am fearfully and wonderfully
    made;
your works are wonderful,
I know that full well.

My frame was not hidden from you
when I was made in the secret place.
When I was woven together in the depths of the
    earth,
your eyes saw my unformed body.
All the days ordained for me
were written in your book
before one of them came to be.

PSALM 139:13–16

Lord, my friend is tired and worried. He knows You love him.
He knows You hear and answer his prayers. However many
days You have ordained for him to live, may he live them in
wonder of Your works. Thank You for his life. Thank You for his
health, such as it is. If it be Your will, heal him, but if not, for
however long he has to live, let him rejoice in You, Lord, his
Savior. In Jesus' name I pray. Amen.

---------------◆---------------

STRESS, LIKE SIN, CANNOT BE TAMED
IF IT CANNOT BE NAMED.

CHAPTER FORTY-FIVE

Footprints of Faith

---❖---

I SAID TO MYSELF, "RELAX AND REST.

GOD HAS SHOWERED YOU WITH BLESSINGS.

SOUL, YOU'VE BEEN RESCUED FROM DEATH;

EYE, YOU'VE BEEN RESCUED FROM TEARS;

AND YOU, FOOT, WERE KEPT FROM STUMBLING."

I'M STRIDING IN THE PRESENCE OF GOD,

ALIVE IN THE LAND OF THE LIVING!

I STAYED FAITHFUL, THOUGH BEDEVILED,

AND DESPITE A TON OF BAD LUCK....

I'LL LIFT HIGH THE CUP OF SALVATION—A TOAST TO GOD!

PSALM 116:7–10, 13 (MSG)

Dear friend:

I cannot *prove* that prayer works. I accept its effectiveness through faith, together with extraordinary experiences I have had that confirm my faith but do not prove it.

To put it another way, we are left with impressions that tell us that prayer works. If a large animal left a footprint, we could begin to ascertain the animal's probable identity along with its weight, sex, and height. Much of my faith is based upon impressions as well—the "footprints" of God that I have discovered in Scripture as well as in the world in which I live. Through the lens of faith, I see God's past involvement in the world, and I can see that He is very active in our lives now as well.

Although I cannot *prove* anything substantive about my faith, such as the Virgin Birth or the Resurrection, medical bioscientists have for the past ten or more years analyzed the "footprint of faith" to better understand how and why it is that people of faith live longer, healthier lives than others. Books have been written on the "biology of faith."

Many studies have correlated prayer and the healing of stress-related diseases. Dr. Herbert Benson, of Harvard Medical School, teaches that 60 to 95 percent of visits to primary care physicians are stress related. God did not create us to endure chronic stress. Whether the stress grows out of a onetime, painful experience, such as a divorce, or is constant, low-level stress, it has a negative impact on our health, including our immune systems. Ask yourself these questions: In the past, what has been the primary source of my stress? Right now, what are my current sources of stress?

Stress, like sin, cannot be tamed if it cannot be named. If you can identify a past source of stress that has made you sick, write a letter to that source. Externalize it. Get it outside of you. Keeping anger or sadness *within* requires a lot of energy and adds stress to our lives. If there is a current source of stress that can be avoided, I would encourage you to do so. Now is not the time for you to be stressed out. Now is the time for you to relax, rest, and remember that "GOD has showered you with blessings."

Develop the calming habit of turning your stress over to God. Jesus instructed us to cast all our burdens on Him; identify your stresses to Him in prayer, ask and trust Him to remove them from your mind and heart and body, and He will lighten your load.

Lord, I know You have showered my friend with blessings. You have left impressions of Your love all around her, including in her heart. Help her now, before it is too late, to rid herself of as much stress as possible so that her immune system will be able to detect and destroy her unwanted cancer. In Jesus' name I pray. Amen

---❖---

I HAVE GOOD NEWS FOR YOU: GOD BLESSES
"THOSE WHO HAVE NOT SEEN AND YET HAVE BELIEVED."

CHAPTER FORTY-SIX

The Faith-Health Connection

❖

"BLESSED ARE THOSE WHO HAVE NOT SEEN AND YET HAVE BELIEVED."

JOHN 20:29

Dear friend:

This morning I noticed that you perked up when I began to share with you some of the scientific evidence relating to the physical benefits of faith in God. Of course, we ought to believe in God apart from what scientists have learned. However, most Christians are like you and me: we believe in God, particularly when scientists validate what the Bible teaches, but we are often like Thomas, who would believe in the Resurrection only if he could touch the risen Jesus. It is in our nature to want evidence. So here is some scientific evidence for you, summarized from Dr. Harold G. Koenig's excellent book *The Healing Power of Faith.*[11]

The overwhelming scientific evidence is that those who have an intrinsic faith or belief system (i.e., those who *really* believe in God, who put faith into action through prayer, regular worship attendance, service to others, etc.) benefit enormously from their faith.

- Statistically, they live seven years longer.
- They heal more quickly from their diseases.
- The length of their hospital stays is significantly shorter.
- The medication needed is often reduced.
- Stress-related diseases are diminished.
- Cortisol levels are lower.
- IgA levels are enhanced.
- CD4 levels are often increased.
- Interleuken-6 levels are lower.

In sum, an intrinsic religious faith helps people live longer, healthier lives *if* their faith is placed in an all-powerful, personal, responsive, loving, just, forgiving, immensely merciful, and understanding God. I believe that description of God reflects the attributes of the Trinity: Father, Son, and Holy Spirit.

A word of caution: If you do not believe, all the evidence in the world will not make you a believer. It will only, perhaps, make you want to mimic the things believers do in hopes of experiencing the benefits they experience. However, if you do believe, I have good news for you: God blesses "those who have not seen and yet have believed." And, the evidence clearly demonstrates, He often does so with longer life and better health.

I hope that good news perks you up today.

Lord Jesus, forgive our Thomas-like doubting, but thank You for all of the faith-affirming scientific evidence that confirms that You are the Author and Sustainer of life. Continue to sustain my friend's life today, I pray, in Jesus' name. Amen.

CHAPTER FORTY-SEVEN

Patience—Simple, Really

---◆---

IN ALL THE TRAVELS OF THE ISRAELITES, WHENEVER
THE CLOUD LIFTED FROM ABOVE THE TABERNACLE, THEY WOULD
SET OUT; BUT IF THE CLOUD DID NOT LIFT, THEY DID NOT SET
OUT—UNTIL THE DAY IT LIFTED.

EXODUS 40:36–37

Dear friend:

I have a confession to make: I am not a very patient person. After our conversation today, something tells me that I am not alone.

My own journey toward learning how to be more patient began with contemplating the great spiritual lessons that the people of Israel learned while they were wandering in the wilderness. They learned to wait upon God's direction and leadership. Have you?

Let God direct. When the cloud is down, be patient and wait. When it rises, move. It's simple, really. When it is time to move, God will make it apparent to His people, including you and me.

And yet, as simple as this lesson seems, putting it into practice is altogether another thing.

One day I asked God to help me learn to be patient. I was anxiety ridden. As clearly as God has ever spoken to me, He said, "Michael, you have your health. Your finances are sufficient. Your family is without serious problems. Your ministry is doing well. There is only one cross I am asking you to carry, only one burden I am asking you to bear, only one lesson I want you to learn: be patient and trust Me to lead and direct your life."

Bearing a cross is a biblical metaphor for carrying a particular burden. In addition to other difficulties you may have, God has a cross for you as well. Be patient. Wait. In His perfect timing, God will lead and direct you in accordance with His perfect will.

Lord Jesus Christ, my friend is tired of waiting. He waits for test results. He waits for the doctor to come. He waits for the chemotherapy to rid him of cancer. He waits for the nausea to leave. His whole life seems to be waiting, waiting, waiting. Help him to carry his cross, as heavy as it may sometimes feel. Teach him the lesson of the wilderness. Remind him that when it is time to move, You will make that apparent to him—when the cloud is down, he should be patient and wait; when it rises, he should move. Lord, lead and direct his life in accordance with Your perfect will. Amen.

CHAPTER FORTY-EIGHT

Reconnecting with God

---❖---

IF I HAVE THE GIFT OF PROPHECY AND CAN FATHOM ALL
MYSTERIES AND ALL KNOWLEDGE, AND IF I HAVE A FAITH THAT
CAN MOVE MOUNTAINS, BUT HAVE NOT LOVE, I AM NOTHING.

1 CORINTHIANS 13:2

D ear friend:
At the Spirituality and Health seminar the other
day, you told the class that you are not sure you believe
in God. I trust that you felt respected and understood by those of
us who, for the most part, claim a Christian heritage. The fact
that you came to the class suggests that during your cancer treatment you are asking yourself some *ultimate* questions: "Is there a
God? If so, can God cure my cancer? If I die, what happens
next?" These are common questions for obvious reasons.

Here are two key principles I've learned during my ministry
that may help you find the answers you are searching for.

1. Every religion in the world, including the Christian religion, is multifaceted in that its adherents range from the very
liberal to the very conservative. Even within one denomination
there is a range of beliefs, though obviously the areas of

disagreement are narrowed. So, for example, when someone tells me that she is a Christian, it means very little to me. I wonder, *What kind of Christian is she? What does she believe?* The answers you will receive to your questions will vary according to the point of view of the source of the information.

2. Adding to the confusion, the religious language people use does not always mean the same thing; often, important words like *spirituality* and *salvation* do not have a common meaning. For example, *spirituality* is not a biblical word. A biblical word search on my computer yielded this result: "Sorry, we found no verses matching your specifications."

Let me explain what I believe this word means from a biblical perspective. The word *religion* comes from the Latin word *religio*, which means "to religament." If a leg or arm became dislocated, it would need to be religamented, or reconnected. Most of the world's religions claim that following their doctrines reconnects the creature to the Creator—the relationship is restored. Islam claims this reconnection through adherence to the Quran and its teachings. Jews claim reconnection through the covenant God manifested to Abraham. Christians claim to be reconnected through the cross. The sacrificial death of Jesus on the cross made necessary by the sinfulness of the world, including your sins and mine, relays this simple message to all who would believe: you are forgiven. All is restored. Come home.

Religion connects people to God. Spirituality, on the other hand, consists of the things believers do to maintain the connection, to ensure the vibrancy of the restored relationship. Among other things, Christian spirituality consists of reading the Bible; praying; worshiping; serving the less fortunate; taking care of one's body; and, most of all, loving others as God, in Christ, loves us. The Scriptures of the Old and New Testaments are my primary source of information about God. I enjoy reading books by well-meaning authors, but if what they have to say isn't grounded in the Word of God, I have little interest in what they have to share.

As you continue asking questions and probing your faith, my guess is that you feel disconnected from God. If you would like to be reconnected to the God whom Christians claim is fully revealed in Jesus Christ, you might begin with God's desire to be reconnected with you. God will not force His will upon you, but He does invite you to accept His love. Jesus said,

> "I am the gate; whoever enters through me will be saved. He will come in and go out, and find pasture. The thief comes only to steal and kill and destroy; I came that they may have life, and have it to the full.
>
> "I am the good shepherd. The good shepherd lays down his life for the sheep."
>
> JOHN 10:9–11

I believe Him. I invite you to do the same. After all, He came that we might have life.

Lord, my friend is searching. When she is ready to enter through the door, take her hand and help her to live—today— for You. In Jesus' name I pray. Amen.

---◆---

"As long as you are living, there is an
opportunity to survive," he explained. "If you
don't get hope from your doctor, fire your doctor."

CHAPTER FORTY-NINE

Getting Up When You're Down

------------------ ❖ ------------------

"WHAT STRENGTH DO I HAVE, THAT I SHOULD STILL HOPE?
WHAT PROSPECTS, THAT I SHOULD BE PATIENT?"

JOB 6:11

Dear friend:
You asked me what happened to the person with colon cancer—if I had seen him lately and, if so, how he was doing. Because the hospital has strict confidentiality restrictions, I am not able to tell you specific details. But I can tell you a story.

Once upon a time there was a man who had enjoyed a wonderful life that included many children and grandchildren and a wonderful career. A baseball-sized tumor was removed from his colon, and he faced Stage 4 colon cancer that had spread to both lobes of his liver. His surgeon told him that chemotherapy could keep him alive for a short time, but that statistically he had between six months and two years left to live. The doctor confided to his family that it would be closer to four months.

This man wasn't ready to die, nor did he like the stark prediction of certain death. "As long as you are living, there is an opportunity to survive," he explained. "If you don't get hope from your doctor, fire your doctor," he now tells those who ask for advice.

He researched his options and discovered a Stage 3 clinical trial. He enrolled in the program. His fifty-fifty chance of getting an experimental drug fueled his hopes for recovery. For good measure, he invented his own cancer-zapping computer game. With help from a hospital social worker who was studying visualization, the man loaded scans of his liver into his home computer. "I was deep into looking at the tumors every day on my computer," he said. "I had my liver scans, and I erased the tumors on my liver." He would also print the scans and laboriously erase the dark ink of the tumors or carefully scrape them off the paper with a razor blade. "You have to develop something to get you up when you're down. You have to take action," he said.

About six weeks later, a new scan of his liver showed that the tumors were significantly smaller. His oncologist called it remarkable and said she'd never seen such a dramatic reduction in cancer. His doctor noted, "He used everything from both ends of the spectrum—traditional scientific treatment and the complete other side, like prayer, forgiveness, contacting people from the past, things that are psychically good ... things that can't be measured."

"We don't necessarily have to be a statistic," the man said. "I believe the medical folks treat us for the disease, but they don't teach us how to survive. We must learn that for ourselves."

An article was written about this man. The headline read, "Colon Cancer Survivor Proves Doctors Wrong."[12]

I believe the man you asked about will likely be telling a similar story soon.

Father in heaven, help my friend to use all of the means of grace available through science, as well as those things that cannot be measured, such as prayer, forgiveness, and contacting people from the past with whom he has painful unfinished business. Whatever it takes, Lord, help him do it for his family, for his future, and for You. In Jesus' name I pray. Amen.

———————— ❖ ————————

YOU NEED TO KNOW THAT YOU ARE AN INSPIRATION
TO ME AND TO MANY OTHERS.

————————————————

CHAPTER FIFTY

Permission to Be Human

---❖---

PETER SAID, "MASTER, I'M READY FOR ANYTHING WITH YOU.
I'D GO TO JAIL FOR YOU. I'D DIE FOR YOU!" JESUS SAID,
"I'M SORRY TO HAVE TO TELL YOU THIS, PETER,
BUT BEFORE THE ROOSTER CROWS YOU WILL
HAVE THREE TIMES DENIED THAT YOU KNOW ME."

LUKE 22:33–34 (MSG)

Dear friend:
One of these days I am going to write a book titled *Everything I Ever Needed to Know I Learned from Cancer Patients*. And I'm going to dedicate it to you. Although I wish I could wave a magic wand over you and make you well, you need to know that you are an inspiration to me and to many others. Here are some of the unforgettable lessons I've learned from you:

1. It is important to trust in God's love without doubt.
2. Life is precious. Don't take one day for granted.
3. Good friends are lifesavers.
4. Self-care begins with reducing as much stress as possible.
5. Some pain is necessary.

6. Healing emotional wounds is critical for healthy living.

7. Forgiveness brings hope for a new and healthier life.

8. Life-threatening disease reveals a person's true character.

9. Love is the most powerful force in the universe.

10. Feeling alone may be the best and worst part of coping with disease.

11. Allow friends, family, and loved ones to be human—to let you down, even when you need them the most.

Of the things I just listed, the last one must be the hardest to learn. I was sad when you told me that some of your family members are afraid of your illness, that they treat you as though you have a contagious disease. It is true that some people do not know much about cancer. They do not know what to say and therefore live in fear that they might say the wrong thing. Some people continue to believe that cancer is a fatal disease. Some people simply do not like being in a hospital or being around those who are sick. They have their own phobias, and although their fears are not based upon reality, that is the way they are, and we know they are not likely to change.

It is important to understand them. You need to accept what they have to give and learn that your friends, as much as you love them, have their own limits of helpfulness. You need to have the spiritual maturity to allow your dearest friends to disappoint you.

Continue to communicate your needs to your family and friends. Give them permission to feel their feelings and think their thoughts—to be human, complete with strengths and weaknesses.

Even Jesus felt abandoned by His disciples in His hour of need. The disciples finally came around. I hope your friends

will come around too. You are an amazing witness of unconditional love, and I admire your faith.

*Lord, sometimes our friends and family let us down when we
need them the most. Help us to grant them a special measure of
grace, even as You understood that Your friends would not be
there for You when You needed them the most. Help my friend
to be reasonable in her expectations of what people can and
cannot do for her. In Jesus' name I pray. Amen.*

———————————— ❖ ————————————

BE AWARE THAT IT IS POSSIBLE FOR GOODNESS
TO COME OUT OF THIS NIGHTMARE.

————————————————————————

CHAPTER FIFTY-ONE

Medical Negligence

---◆---

"AWAY WITH THE NOISE OF YOUR SONGS!
I WILL NOT LISTEN TO THE MUSIC OF YOUR HARPS.
BUT LET JUSTICE ROLL ON LIKE A RIVER,
RIGHTEOUSNESS LIKE A NEVER-FAILING STREAM!"

AMOS 5:23–24

Dear friend:

You have experienced everyone's worst nightmare. I am groping for the right words to say and finding it very hard to control my own anger. How can a laboratory repeatedly misread pap smears over a period of three years? What must it feel like to know that the cancer you developed could have been prevented if the people who read the tests had detected the abnormalities? Isn't that why women get pap smears in the first place? And now, because of the hysterectomy, you cannot have children. Your life, your marriage, your hopes and dreams— victimized. How is it possible to right this wrong?

You asked me what you should do. In light of what appears to be gross negligence, this is how I would handle the situation:

1. I would not sue. I would forgive. However, my forgiveness would include a demand that the hospital and laboratory prove that they have made whatever changes are necessary to ensure that the mistake will never happen again.

2. I would invite the hospital to address my situation, trusting that, if given the opportunity, it would do the right thing by responding to my need in a humanitarian way.

3. I would seek counseling to deal with the rage I was feeling, inasmuch as my understandable anger would have a negative impact upon my immune system.

4. I would ask God to allow justice to "roll on like a river" and "righteousness like a never-failing stream" so that the lives of others would be spared of this pain.

5. Lastly, I would commit myself to spreading the word about the importance of getting second opinions. As you mentioned, the lesson you learned is the message everyone needs to hear before there are problems: get second opinions. Have test results double-checked, even if it costs a little more.

Be aware that it is possible for goodness to come out of this nightmare. Trust God to work in and through your tragedy. Whatever you do, don't let this go unnoticed.

Father in heaven, I ask for justice for my friend—on Your terms and not her own. Please show her how she can be reassured that "all things work together for good" (Rom. 8:28 KJV), because right now she is unable to even imagine how goodness can come out of this nightmare. Give her peace. In Jesus' name I pray. Amen.

CHAPTER FIFTY-TWO

The Aroma of Christ

❖

FOR WE ARE TO GOD THE AROMA OF CHRIST AMONG THOSE WHO
ARE BEING SAVED AND THOSE WHO ARE PERISHING.

2 CORINTHIANS 2:15

D ear friend:

The smells are unmistakable, aren't they? You notice nothing unusual in the lobby. Or in the restaurant. Or on the elevator. It is even normal on the oncology floor in the hospital. And then, as you enter the outpatient wing, the aroma of the chemicals tells you that, as "homey" as the atmosphere may be, there are sick people here, and in some cases they are very sick.

It serves as an instant reminder that you are sick too. The smell, you said, triggered fear and flooded you with anxiety to the point where you felt nauseated, and the washroom to which you retreated gave no relief from the smells. I am glad to hear that you now bring with you some handkerchiefs on which you sprinkle essential oils such as peppermint or grapefruit. Good smells are soothing and therapeutic.

The Bible teaches us that "we are to God the aroma of Christ among those who are being saved and those who are perishing." God apparently is sensitive to smell too.

When people are around us, is our aroma as Christians hopeful? Or is it the aroma of pessimism and despair? Are we depressing to be around? Or do we exude confidence and trust in God's love?

You have the choice to be the aroma of Christ or the aroma of misery. If you need some help in learning how to be the aroma of Christ, especially when you are feeling lousy, consider a different metaphor: imagine a tapestry. The back of the tapestry displays a jumbled compilation of threads with no apparent pattern. There are different colors, different sizes of thread, big ugly knots. You see hanging, drooping combinations of warp and weft that appear to exhibit the mindless creativity of a child. Turn the tapestry over, however, and there is a work of art—neatly patterned and beautiful.

As Christians we believe that "all things work together for good to them that love God, to them who are the called according to his purpose" (Rom. 8:28 KJV). Although our sinful human nature is innately attracted to that which is unlovely and negative, we can choose to look at our situations from the human, ugly side or from the beautifully patterned side, the side that God views.

If you hope to be the fragrant aroma of Christ, focus on how God is using your chemotherapy to heal you. The outpatient clinic need not be perceived as an ugly, smelly, and unavoidable place but as the most beautiful place on the earth, a place where God is palpably present and where healing takes place.

Which side of the tapestry are you going to focus on today? The side you choose as your focal point will largely determine whether you are the aroma of Christ or the stench of hopelessness and despair.

Lord, whenever my friend begins to think negative, unlovely thoughts, help him to quickly turn his thoughts to the lovely side of the tapestry of life. It is easier said than done, so he will need Your help—and often. As he battles cancer, help him to be the aroma of Christ to all who are around him every day. In Jesus' name I pray. Amen.

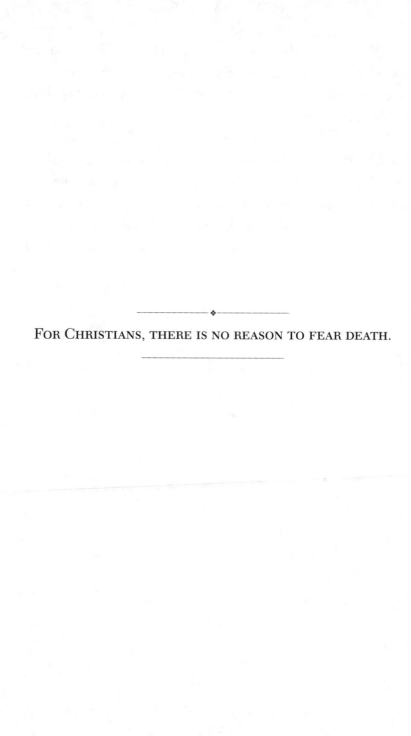

FOR CHRISTIANS, THERE IS NO REASON TO FEAR DEATH.

CHAPTER FIFTY-THREE

Fighting for Life
but Obedient to Death

❖

FOR TO ME, TO LIVE IS CHRIST AND TO DIE IS GAIN.

PHILIPPIANS 1:21

D ear friend:
    You caught me off guard this afternoon when
    you asked me about death. I spend so much time
thinking about life and living that thinking about death and
dying seems abnormal. After all, the focus of my ministry is
health and healing, finding ways to integrate our faith in Christ
into the healing equation. I treat death as though it were something to be avoided at all cost. And yet, I really don't believe
that death, in and of itself, is the villain. The villain is *premature*
death, not death itself.

Paul often felt conflicted about life and living. He believed
that it was possible for him to exalt Christ in his body, "whether
by life or by death" (Phil. 1:20). In the end, living our lives for
Christ, whether our paths lead to life and health or dying and
death, seems to be the appropriate attitude to have.

Jesus "became obedient to death" (Phil. 2:8). I take that to
mean that there will be a time in each of our lives when death

will need to be obeyed. God has promised that, when our time has come to die, He personally will take His children to be with Him (see John 14:3). When we become convinced that it is now time to "become obedient to death," we must let go, give up, prepare for the journey from this life to the life that is to come—living eternally with God. No one can tell you when that moment is. The decision to give up the fight for life is probably the most personally intimate decision a person can make. It is a moment that crystallizes a person's values, hopes, dreams, and faith.

The Scriptures teach us, however, that there is a time to live and a time to die (see Eccl. 3:1–3). Death, it would appear, can be held off through the best efforts of loved ones, health professionals, and our own desire to struggle for life. This is our reality.

I choose to fight for life because Jesus valued life. He healed frequently. He came to give us abundant life (see John 10:10). By His Spirit He sustains our life. I choose to be obedient to life and its Author.

Fearing death creates stress and anxiety, which may be counterproductive to regaining your health. For Christians, there is no reason to fear death. My advice? Be obedient to life. Fight for it. Struggle to overcome any disease that threatens it. Exhaust yourself until it comes time to be obedient to death.

Lord, for us, to live is Christ and to die is gain. Whatever happens, may my friend conduct himself "in a manner worthy of the gospel of Christ" (Phil. 1:27). Amen.

CHAPTER FIFTY-FOUR

The Litmus Test of Love

---◆---

IF ANYONE SAYS, "I LOVE GOD," YET HATES HIS BROTHER,
HE IS A LIAR. FOR ANYONE WHO DOES NOT LOVE HIS BROTHER,
WHOM HE HAS SEEN, CANNOT LOVE GOD, WHOM HE HAS NOT SEEN.
AND HE HAS GIVEN US THIS COMMAND: WHOEVER LOVES GOD
MUST ALSO LOVE HIS BROTHER.

1 JOHN 4:20–21

Dear friend:

Mitch Albom has written a book titled *The Five People You Meet in Heaven*. While he is not pretending to offer anything more than a good read and some good advice, I have to tell you that it is not the five people we will meet *in heaven* who matter the most but rather the five people we meet *on earth* who determine whether we will ever be allowed to enter heaven in the first place.

The first person, of course, is *Jesus Christ*. According to the Scriptures, we have no hope of heaven apart from faith in Him alone. Rejecting Jesus in this life precludes any hope for eternal life with God (see John 14:1–7). Assuming that we say we love the Lord, Jesus introduces us to four other people to determine whether we truly love Him in our hearts or are fooling ourselves. These four people serve as a litmus test of our love for Him.

The first person Jesus introduces us to is the *neighbor.* To love Jesus is to love our neighbors as ourselves, and He helps us understand that "neighbor" does not simply include family members, friends, or other Christians, but anyone in need. This is the lesson of the Parable of the Good Samaritan (see Luke 10:25–37).

The second person Jesus introduces us to is the *poor.* To love Jesus is to love "the least of these" (Matt. 25:40)—the poor, the imprisoned, the hungry, the homeless. To turn away from the needs of the desperate and the destitute is to deny our love for Jesus (see Matt. 25:31–46).

The third person Jesus introduces us to is the *enemy.* To love Jesus is to love our enemies. In the Sermon on the Mount, Jesus teaches the gathered crowd that to be His disciple, one must love one's enemies. "Bless them; do not curse them," He teaches (Matt. 5:44).

The fourth and final person Jesus introduces us to is *ourselves.* How obscene it is, in light of God's sacrifice of His Son, to hate the one He chose to die for: *you.* God loves you. You are worthy of His love because He has made you worthy (see John 3:16).

To love Jesus is to meet and love who Jesus loved. He loved His neighbor. He loved the poor. He loved and forgave His enemies.

He loves you.

Father, help my friend to see the face of his neighbor in the bed across the room. Help him to forgive and to bless those who have hurt him. Help him to reach out in love and compassion to those who need a helping hand or an encouraging word. And help him to value himself because You love him. In Jesus' name I pray. Amen.

CHAPTER FIFTY-FIVE

Singing the Lord's Song

❖

THEN HE SAID TO ME, "PROPHESY TO THESE BONES AND SAY TO
THEM, 'DRY BONES, HEAR THE WORD OF THE LORD! THIS IS WHAT
THE SOVEREIGN LORD SAYS TO THESE BONES: I WILL MAKE
BREATH ENTER YOU, AND YOU WILL COME TO LIFE. I WILL ATTACH
TENDONS TO YOU AND MAKE FLESH COME UPON YOU AND COVER
YOU WITH SKIN; I WILL PUT BREATH IN YOU, AND YOU WILL COME
TO LIFE. THEN YOU WILL KNOW THAT I AM THE LORD.'"

EZEKIEL 37:4–6

Dear friend:
We know each other too well to pretend that
there is a single reason to be hopeful about your
recovery. Today, nothing seems to be going your way. You have
waged a faithful, valiant fight against cancer, and now the end
seems certain—and near. Hope has ebbed and is beginning to
give way to hopelessness.

You have the right to give up, and if you do, no one will
hold that against you. And yet, I want to be the face of love and
hope to you, even when it seems as though we are hoping

against hope. The Bible speaks of others who have been hopeless. For example, remember the exiles in Babylon?

When the promising young Israelites were dragged into exile in Babylon, they were not kept in prisons or even in camps. They were free to marry, build homes, plant crops, and exchange goods. But the Israelites had a hard time worshiping in exile because they never got over the destruction of their Holy City and the temple in Zion. They were not where they wanted or were supposed to be. So they lived with a sadness that ran down to their bones. And they refused to "sing the songs of the LORD while in a foreign land" (Ps. 137:4).

One day the Spirit of the Lord grabbed hold of His prophet Ezekiel and took him to a valley filled with dry bones. The Lord asked Ezekiel, "Mortal, can these bones live?" (see Ezek. 37:3). Looking around at all those skeletons, Ezekiel thought hard and said, "Ah, Lord, You know the answer to this one" (see 37:3). Then the Lord told him to start preaching to the bones. The Lord even gave him the message: "Dry bones, hear the word of the LORD! This is what the Sovereign LORD says to these bones: 'I will make breath enter you, and you will come to life.... Then you will know that I am the LORD.'"

As Rev. Dr. Craig Barnes once said:

So we will take our stand beside Ezekiel and proclaim our hope to the dry bones, "Thus, says the Lord, I will cause breath to enter you and you shall live!" You who gave up hope, who gave up dreaming—who have settled for a comfortably routine life of work, bills and dirty laundry. You who think your best years are behind you. You who think the Lord God has forgotten all about your little life. To you, we say, "Arise!" Arise from the heap of discarded dreams. Arise to discover that the Holy Spirit is breathing hope back into you.[13]

You may wake up tomorrow in heaven, or you may still be here with the rest of us. But one thing is certain: God can breathe life into dead bones. If He can do that, perhaps He can breathe hope back into you and me and all those who love you dearly.

Father, You are our only hope. Try as hard as we might, we can't seem to find any good reason for hope, save some miraculous divine intervention. God, my friend needs You today. Hear her cries for help and hope. Regardless of what happens, in the face of hopelessness, help her sing the Lord's song. In Jesus' name I pray. Amen.

---❖---

IT IS TIME FOR YOU TO *PUT IT ALL ON THE LINE* **WITH GOD.**

CHAPTER FIFTY-SIX

Prayer That Risks

---◆---

"ANSWER ME, O LORD, ANSWER ME, SO THESE PEOPLE WILL KNOW
THAT YOU, O LORD, ARE GOD, AND THAT YOU ARE TURNING THEIR
HEARTS BACK AGAIN." THEN THE FIRE OF THE LORD FELL AND
BURNED UP THE SACRIFICE, THE WOOD, THE STONES AND THE
SOIL, AND ALSO LICKED UP THE WATER IN THE TRENCH. WHEN ALL
THE PEOPLE SAW THIS, THEY FELL PROSTRATE AND CRIED, "THE
LORD—HE IS GOD! THE LORD—HE IS GOD!"

1 KINGS 18:37–39

Dear friend:

You asked me to pray for your healing, and I was
honored to do so. As I told you, if you are not healed
of your cancer, it will not be because together we did not
fervently, faithfully, and boldly ask God for healing.

Jesus said, "Ask and you will receive" (John 16:24). Jesus
said it; I believe it. For me, it is that simple. The ball, so to
speak, is in God's court. Like Elijah, I put it all on the line.
Surrounded by 450 prophets of Baal, he prayed that the Lord
God would hear his prayer. He drenched the wood three times
and then asked God to consume it by fire. Following his faithful

prayer, "the fire of the LORD fell and burned up the sacrifice, the wood, the stones and the soil, and also licked up the water in the trench." Elijah put it all on the line by trusting God to do something miraculous.

I read a short story recently by Robert Huffman titled "A Question of Rain." The story is about a pastor who was asked by many people in his town to pray for rain. Although there had been a severe drought and the people's lives had been devastated, the pastor did not want to pray for rain for fear that God would not answer his prayer and he would feel like a fool. He didn't want to "put it all on the line." He gave in, however, and held a prayer service. Sure enough, as he headed home afterward, it rained.

It is time for you to *put it all on the line* with God. Pray for healing. James, the brother of Jesus, taught us to put it all on the line when he said:

> Is any one of you in trouble? He should pray. Is anyone happy? Let him sing songs of praise. Is any one of you sick? He should call the elders of the church to pray over him and anoint him with oil in the name of the Lord. And the prayer offered in faith will make the sick person well; the Lord will raise him up.
>
> JAMES 5:13–15

Noah put it all on the line; he built the ark when there wasn't a cloud in the sky. Elijah put it all on the line so that "these people will know that you, O LORD, are God, and that you are turning their hearts back again." Jesus put it all on the line and was raised on the third day.

The Bible says it. I believe it. I invite you to believe it as well.

Father, help my friend to put it all on the line, even though prayer for healing may make him feel uncomfortable. Remove his fear of failure, and replace it with a strong trust in Your love for Your people. Heal him, please. For I know that You, O Lord, are God. In Jesus' name I pray. Amen.

—————————— ❖ ——————————

PLEASE KNOW HOW VERY PROUD I AM OF YOU.
PLEASE KNOW THAT I WILL BE AT YOUR SIDE,
PRAYING FOR YOU AND SUPPORTING YOUR FAMILY.

——————————————————————

CHAPTER FIFTY-SEVEN

If the End Appears Near

❖

WHEN THE PERISHABLE HAS BEEN CLOTHED WITH THE IMPERISH-
ABLE, AND THE MORTAL WITH IMMORTALITY, THEN THE SAYING
THAT IS WRITTEN WILL COME TRUE: "DEATH HAS BEEN SWAL-
LOWED UP IN VICTORY." "WHERE, O DEATH, IS YOUR VICTORY?
WHERE, O DEATH, IS YOUR STING?" THE STING OF DEATH IS SIN,
AND THE POWER OF SIN IS THE LAW. BUT THANKS BE TO GOD! HE
GIVES US THE VICTORY THROUGH OUR LORD JESUS CHRIST.

1 CORINTHIANS 15:54–57

Dear friend:

This may be the last letter I write to you—at least while you are living on earth. I felt honored and privileged to be with you this morning as you shared your thoughts—and tears. If today is to be your last, please know how very proud I am of you. If it is not, then as you drift in and out of awareness, please know that I will be at your side, praying for you and supporting your family.

This is what I will say to your children when you are in heaven: "Children, your mother loved you very much, and she was proud of each of you. She is aware that in her final days she did not communicate her love for you as well as she might have. However, she wanted you to know that her last words were about you.

"We talked about each of you before she died. She shared a few memories with me and, in the midst of tears, said that she felt bad that she is not going to be there for you—to celebrate your birthdays, dance at your weddings, and spoil your children.

"She also wanted you to know that, in a strange way, she has made peace with the fact that she is not going to survive her cancer. In spite of her fighting attitude and the valiant effort of so many others, she knew that heaven is her true home and that Jesus was preparing a very special place for her. She believed that this was the time for her reunion with the Lord, her parents, and the loved ones who have gone on before her.

"She asked me to share this with you: Never ask, 'Why?' but only 'Where?' Not 'Why did this happen to her?' but 'Where is she?' In doing so, you can gain a sense of peace and comfort in knowing that as much as you loved her and she loved you, she knew the Lord loved her more.

"Although her cancer diagnosis changed her life, it was not altogether in a negative way. She became a stronger person because of it in all the areas of life where being strong is a virtue. She became enormously strong in her faith. She was strong in her love for life and her desire to live. She gained spiritual strength as she nurtured some of her friends with cancer, giving them encouragement and hope.

"Everyone at the hospital will miss her, and we all feel empty inside, wishing we could have done more to save her. I speak for everyone who became her friend over the past couple of years. We loved your mother very much, and we will miss her too.

"When I asked her what her life's greatest accomplishment was, without hesitation she said it was *you*. She believed that. She loved and believed in you. Remember: Don't ask, 'Why?' just 'Where?' We will never know the answer to the first question, but we are certain of the answer to the last."

Friend, I ask this one favor of you. If it is possible, send an angel to comfort us, for we will all miss you very, very much.

Lord Jesus, the threshold of death is frightening for most of us. And yet the hope of heaven is there for all who trust in Your redeeming love. However long we have to live, make us mindful that we live our lives in the palm of Your hand and that You are Lord of the past, present, and future. In Jesus' name I pray. Amen.

———————— ❖ ————————

TRUST GOD—
IN THE GOOD TIMES AND THE BAD TIMES
AND EVERY MOMENT IN BETWEEN.

————————————————

CHAPTER FIFTY-EIGHT

Last Words

---❖---

"DO NOT LET YOUR HEARTS BE TROUBLED. TRUST IN GOD; TRUST
ALSO IN ME. IN MY FATHER'S HOUSE ARE MANY ROOMS; IF IT WERE
NOT SO, I WOULD HAVE TOLD YOU. I AM GOING THERE TO PREPARE
A PLACE FOR YOU. AND IF I GO AND PREPARE A PLACE FOR YOU, I
WILL COME BACK AND TAKE YOU TO BE WITH ME THAT YOU ALSO
MAY BE WHERE I AM. YOU KNOW THE WAY TO THE PLACE WHERE I
AM GOING." THOMAS SAID TO HIM, "LORD, WE DON'T KNOW WHERE
YOU ARE GOING, SO HOW CAN WE KNOW THE WAY?" JESUS
ANSWERED, "I AM THE WAY AND THE TRUTH AND THE LIFE. NO
ONE COMES TO THE FATHER EXCEPT THROUGH ME. IF YOU REALLY
KNEW ME, YOU WOULD KNOW MY FATHER AS WELL. FROM NOW ON,
YOU DO KNOW HIM AND HAVE SEEN HIM."

JOHN 14:1–7

Dear friend:
This is the last letter I will be writing to you for
awhile. As such, I want this to be the best letter I
could possibly write—the most meaningful; the most helpful,
hopeful, and encouraging.

If I were to have only one sermon left to preach, what passage would I use? If my wife and children were at my bedside as I battled disease or approached death, what would be my words to them? If my grandchildren and great-grandchildren, whom I never knew, had the opportunity to read one letter or hear one of my sermons, how would I want them to think of me?

I want people to know two things. First, that I—pastor, husband, father, grandfather—wholly and completely trusted in God. I trusted in His love, His forgiveness and mercy, His power to heal. I trusted in His power to renew and transform human life into the image of Jesus Christ, thereby making the greedy and selfish person love to give and the godless person desire to serve Him alone.

Trust God—in the good times and the bad times and every moment in between.

Second, I want my legacy to be that I believed and taught that Jesus is the only way to the Father. He alone is heaven's gate. His way is the narrow path. Among the last things I would say at the end of my life (and now to you) would be that heaven is available to all who put their trust in Jesus. If you haven't given your life to Christ, please do so before it is too late. There are many second chances in this life, but there are none in the life to come.

Finally, the last words I hope to speak to my family and friends, including you, are these two words: *Thank you.*

Thank you, my friend, for the privilege of knowing you. Thank you for sharing your deepest thoughts and your heart's greatest hopes and dreams. Thank you for your wonderful attitude and willingness to endure the occasional indignities of life in a hospital in order to get well and live a long, purposeful life. Thank you for strong handshakes, gentle smiles, wet tears, and warm hugs. Thank you for being my friend. Please know that my friendship does not end with your departure from the hospital.

Stay in touch.

Yours in Christ,
MIKE

P.S. Thank you. Thank you. Thank you.

Notes

1 Stephen Jencks, MD, "The Right Care," *New England Journal of Medicine* (May 29, 2003), 225.

2 James Pennebaker, Ph.D., *Writing to Heal: A Guided Journal for Recovering from Trauma & Emotional Upheaval* (Oakland, Calif.: New Harbinger Press, 2004), 146–147.

3 Agnes Sanford, *The Healing Gifts of the Spirit* (San Francisco: HarperSanFrancisco, 1966), 162.

4 See Dr. Alison Fife's research through study at Brigham and Women's Hospital referenced in Dr. Harold Koenig's book *The Healing Power of Faith* (New York: Simon and Schuster, 1999).

5 Sherwin B. Nuland, *How We Die: Reflections on Life's Final Chapter* (New York: Alfred A. Knopf, 1994), 208.

6 Dr. Benson spoke these words as a plenary speaker at a conference entitled "Spirituality and Health," sponsored by the Department of Continuing Education, Harvard Medical School. The seminar was held in Indianapolis, Indiana, in March 2003.

7 Dr. Ralph Moss, "Spontaneous Regressions," *The Moss Reports* (Sept. 11, 2002), http://cancerdecisions.com/091102.html.

8 Dr. Harold Koenig, *The Healing Power of Faith,* 208–209.

9 Ibid., 172.

10 First Corinthians 12:4–11 says:

> There are different kinds of gifts, but the same Spirit. There are different kinds of service, but the same Lord. There are different kinds of working, but the same God works all of them in all men.
>
> Now to each one the manifestation of the Spirit is given for the common good. To one there is given through the Spirit the message of wisdom, to another the message of knowledge by

means of the same Spirit, to another *faith* by the same Spirit, to
another gifts of healing by that one Spirit, to another miraculous
powers, to another prophecy, to another distinguishing between
spirits, to another speaking in different kinds of tongues, and to
still another the interpretation of tongues. All these are the work
of one and the same Spirit, and he gives them to each one, just
as he determines.

11   Dr. Harold Koenig, *The Healing Power of Faith*, 206–230.

12   His story, and many others like it, can be found on the Web site for the
American Cancer Society. Look up the Cancer Survivors Network at
http://www.acscsn.org.

13   Craig Barnes, *When God Interrupts* (Downers Grove, Ill.: InterVarsity Press,
1996).

For More Information

There are fine cancer treatment facilities in hospitals and outpatient clinics across America and around the world, and many facilities believe in a spiritual connection to physical healing from the biblical perspective. Among such facilities are the Cancer Treatment Centers of America, for whom Dr. Barry serves as a chaplain to cancer patients. PHONE: 1-800-FOR-HELP

CANCER TREATMENT CENTERS OF AMERICA
AT MIDWESTERN REGIONAL
MEDICAL CENTER
2520 ELISHA AVENUE
ZION, ILLINOIS 60099

CANCER TREATMENT CENTERS OF AMERICA
AT SOUTHWESTERN REGIONAL
MEDICAL CENTER
10109 EAST 79TH STREET
TULSA, OKLAHOMA 74133

CANCER TREATMENT CENTERS OF AMERICA
AT SEATTLE CANCER TREATMENT AND
WELLNESS CENTER
122 16TH AVENUE EAST
SEATTLE, WASHINGTON 98122

Cancer
Treatment
Centers
of America

Winning the fight against cancer, every day.®